IT'S A SHAME
I CAN'T SHARE

Living with Avoidant Personality Disorder

Jake Ware

First print edition January 2023

Cover design by nskvsky

Some names and identifying details of people
described in this book have been altered to protect
their privacy.

Special thanks to Johnny, Emma, Niels, and Ben

https://www.youtube.com/@JakeAvPD

CONTENTS

INTRODUCTION

Do you hate me as much as I do?

I've never actually asked anyone. But I'm always wondering. Does my brother hate me as much as I hate myself? What about that politely-friendly acquaintance at school? Or the waiter that served us in the restaurant last week? How about that dude I've never spoken to, who glanced at me in public for a split second? Maybe my best friend hates me, too.

Imagine wondering that of everyone you ever see. It's not a question, or even words in my mind—just a constant, gut-wrenching apprehension. If that sounds contrived, or pathetically self-pitying, believe me: I get it. And yet, I can't stop wondering, because I've been through this before. Eventually, inevitably, you'll notice something, anything I say or do, and you'll realize or remember that there's something wrong with me. I wonder what you're thinking, and I also watch, because when I see that realization dawn on your face, for even a moment, I need to leave.

I can't bear to feel the shame of judgment. People talk about growing a "thicker skin", to stop the shame from piercing to your heart. That skin is your ego, your self-esteem; everything you love about yourself in spite of your flaws. That might be your interests or skills, intelligence or dedication, charm or wit. But for some of us, it seems there's nothing there. Yes, the truth hurts. No one enjoys being called out for their shortcomings. But we are meant to take criticism into consideration, and then return to equilibrium, calling to mind our good qualities; remind ourselves that we are more than the missteps that ourselves, or others, perceive.

Some of us can't find our own good qualities. Sometimes we doubt they exist. Other times we're certain they don't. I spent many years hating almost everything about myself. Being criticized crushes me, because it reminds me of what I think I already know to be true. I know how much deeper it goes than the point of criticism itself; it speaks to who I am. I often feel like I have no good in me to shield me from the shame. I'm all too aware of how whiny and exaggerated that sounds, but that's how I've felt for a long time.

You don't have to say it out loud, either. I'll see the judgment in your facial expressions, or your body language, even if it might not mean what I suspect it does. I'm unconsciously keeping track of any way you might react, because I'm terrified that I'll feel that way again: sick, weak-willed, irredeemable—for everyone around to see and feel. Soon enough, I'll see the signs.

Then I'll look for a way out, while it only burns a little bit. I'll think about it for a week straight—how pathetic I was; how stupid it was to force my presence on another person. Every time it's happened before comes burning back into my brain. Eventually, I'll stop coming back. If I just lie to myself that I'd always prefer to be alone, neither I nor anyone else will have to wonder about why I'm so afraid of everything, ever again.

I have avoidant personality disorder, or AvPD. This is what life feels like for me. My intense fear of judgment and criticism makes social interaction truly nauseating, in spite of desiring it for the same reasons anyone else does. At the age of twenty-four, I don't have a social life, or even a job, nor was I able to finish college. I talk only to a few family members, and occasionally online with one friend that I've known for about sixteen years. Until the past few months, I'd rarely even manage to communicate with people online; even through text, even anonymously.

But there's a lot more to it than that. Every human being has their own unique struggles. Some of them are easier to empathize with. Maybe they're more common, more relatable, like having lost a relative. Maybe they're more tangible, their impact more obvious, like a house burning down. Mental health issues are harder. They're completely real, yes, but they really are just in our heads. Even when similar to someone else's, they are unique to us and our experiences.

I want to help you understand AvPD through my insights into myself. Maybe you think you suffer from it, or a friend or family member might. Maybe you're just curious—after all, being better able to understand others opens up possibilities you might never have known about otherwise. No matter who you are, I am anxiously excited to offer you a firsthand account into the symptoms and behavioral changes that are part of AvPD, how they developed in myself throughout my life, how I'm trying to improve and move forward, and, perhaps most importantly, what others might really like to know about getting to know someone with anxiety, or specifically AvPD—like me! Believe me, I would be way too self-conscious to ask anyone to read this if I wasn't pretty sure it was going to be worth their time and effort.

Either way, if there's one thing I would hope you can take away from this: you don't always have to understand what someone else is mentally struggling with. It might make no sense to you at all—what they're dealing with, how it came about, or why they can't seem to shake it—even with their explanation. Just remember, that person probably doesn't expect you to develop a solution to their problems. They just need a friend—to listen to them, and most of all, to trust them.

I'm going to make it. I promised that to myself when I decided to write this book—about how I've made it so far, in spite of not always wanting to. With any luck, this will only be the first step. So let's get the hell on with it, shall we?

AVOIDANCE COMES IN THREES

Before I get into the history of my development of avoidant personality disorder, I want to explain what exactly it is, from a combination of personal experience, and talking online to others with AvPD. But this isn't supposed to read like a psychology textbook, so I'll start with an introduction.

My name is Jake, and I'm a twenty-four year-old dude at the time I'm writing this. I'm a big fan of listening to, playing, and writing metal music—don't knock it till you try it; there's like a hundred subgenres, and only some of the good ones involve people screaming in your ears. My main instrument is bass guitar, played with a pick specifically to annoy fingerstyle players (the awesome accentuation doesn't hurt, either). When I can focus on it, I enjoy writing, particularly young adult fantasy. I'm pretty good at cooking, and I like long, contemplative walks in quiet places. I love video games, specifically an odd combination of fantasy adventure-type stuff, and competitive multiplayer games—which are like sports, but on a computer, and with gear that's arguably even cooler than cleats or golf clubs. My non-specific and purely theoretical dream job is to work as a character moveset designer on a MOBA (*multiplayer online battle arena*) or fighting game, which basically entails deciding how the people that play the game get to virtually beat each other up.

Now that you've most likely developed a highly stereotypical mental image of your narrator, let's talk about AvPD. It's a disorder which affects men and women equally. Most estimates place it as affecting around 2.5% of the adult population in America. Some estimates are even higher—it's hard to be sure, since those suffering have difficulty seeking treatment—yet you might never have heard of it. Even if you have, the limited information available online, while often fairly accurate, is rarely very detailed. I want to provide that detail throughout this whole book. But first, I want to address a couple common points of confusion I've seen in online information and discussions of AvPD.

For one thing, there are some things which AvPD is *not*, but is often conflated with. Two of these are especially problematic, sometimes even in psychiatric-adjacent literature. The first is what's called the avoidant attachment style. This essentially refers to a personality type in which the person hasn't learned how to connect with others, and as such tends to be distant. They might not know how to show or discuss their emotions, or what to do when someone else shows their own. They tend to prefer autonomy over their lives, and may not see making compromises to their own preferences to sustain relationships as being worth it. They might be ambivalent when others would be emotional. While the naming overlap is an obvious reason for confusion, and avoidant attachment style can have some similarities with AvPD, there are parts of it which are, or could be, different from how AvPD presents in people, and there are many elements of AvPD not present with avoidant attachment style. As an attachment style—not a personality disorder, or diagnosis of any kind—it bears much more similarity to something like a four-letter personality type described by the popular Myers-Briggs Type Indicator system than it does to AvPD.

Then, there are the other nine personality disorders. A personality disorder (PD), to quote the DSM-5 (the current American professional standard for mental disorder diagnosis), is "an enduring pattern of inner experience and behavior that deviates markedly from the expectations of the individual's culture". There are similarities between the personality disorders—for one thing, the DSM-5 outlines a set of criteria which must be met to be diagnosed with any one of the specific PDs. The aforementioned "pattern", the symptoms specific to each PD, must manifest itself in at least two of four categories: *cognition* (perception of self, others, or events), *affectivity* (range, intensity, rate of change, and appropriateness of emotional response), *interpersonal functioning*, and *impulse control*. AvPD generally affects the first three of these categories.

The pattern must be inflexible and pervasive throughout a wide range of personal and social situations, causing significant distress or impairment in functioning (particularly social or occupational), consistent over multiple years starting no later than young adulthood, and not better explained by another mental disorder, medical condition, or substance use. There can be some overlap between the specific symptoms of the disorders—the content of these "patterns". For example, people diagnosed with AvPD often show traits of paranoid personality disorder and/or dependent personality disorder. This is sometimes to the severity that they receive an additional diagnosis, though that was not the case for me.

However, "people with any personality disorder" do not have anything implicitly in common with their personalities—yet some people seem to conflate "having a personality disorder" with particular negative traits, like irrationality and anger. Many people are only aware of certain PDs, such as borderline personality disorder (BPD) and narcissistic personality disorder (NPD). This is understandable to an extent— these PDs might be more outwardly evident than some of the others, as part of the Cluster B, or "dramatic" personality disorders.

But there are also those PDs in Cluster A—dubbed "odd"—and Cluster C—labeled "anxious", including AvPD. Each cluster is a group of disorders which present very differently from those in the other clusters, and even within the clusters, each disorder affects personality in a very different way. Most importantly, even people with the same personality disorder are still individuals with unique personalities. While any PD will present those that suffer it with difficulties, it does not mean that those people are bad or mean. Negative stereotypes you might have heard about people with a certain personality disorder might not be true at all, but definitely can't be assumed to be true for anyone with *any* PD.

Besides the other personality disorders, there are still more mental disorders that might be confused with AvPD (and I did so myself before learning about AvPD), but for now, let's focus on what AvPD actually is. Don't worry, it's still plenty complicated on its own; what you might have read online probably does not quite do it justice. Let's break it into three parts: causes, symptoms, and maladaptations.

A helpful, somewhat simplified way of looking at it is to see these three parts as a cycle. *Causes* are uncontrollable, usually external, forces which change our brain function, causing symptoms. *Symptoms* are the proverbial meat-and-potatoes of the disorder, which make life more of a pain in the ass for people that have it. *Maladaptations* are things our brain tells us to do to avoid or lessen the symptoms, which have their own negative side effects. They're the way we've learned to act in response to how much the symptoms suck. They are secondary symptoms in their own right, and they're the sort of things that you'll notice when viewing someone with AvPD from an outside perspective. These maladaptations often put us in scenarios that reinforce our beliefs about ourselves, acting as new causes! That intensifies our symptoms, and we often try to protect ourselves with more maladaptation...you get the idea. That's a feedback loop, and there are a whole bunch of them in AvPD.

There can be quite a bit of variance in each part between different people with AvPD. My particular genetics and experiences determine the causes, which shape the symptoms, and the maladaptations I make to avoid them. I'll speak chiefly to my own causes, symptoms, and maladaptations, but I'll also share some possible differences I've learned about in talking to others with the disorder. I will mostly describe symptoms and maladaptations for now; as you will see, the causes are quite simple to understand on a theoretical level, but unique to each individual in practice, so I will mention them more later when I share my specific experiences.

ANXIETY

The most major symptom is an extreme and particular form of social anxiety. It is my belief that anyone with AvPD could also be diagnosed with social anxiety disorder (as I was, before I even knew what AvPD was), but AvPD explains why it's so specific, intense, and persistent, and does not apply to everyone with social anxiety, even if it's to the extent of being considered a disorder. I feel that I have virtually no redeeming characteristics, and so I default to believing that everyone else will feel that way about me, too. I always feel that I'm unintentionally making other people uncomfortable when I'm around—whether it's with something I say or do, or even my mere presence, posture, body language, or appearance. It makes me feel horrible to make other people feel uncomfortable, and when—not if—I believe I've done so, it only provides me further proof that my existence is a negative one. This, on its own, causes anxiety so extreme that, for years, I have avoided all social interaction as much as possible. In short, it's about avoiding the feeling of shame.

During the past six years or so, since dropping out of college after one semester, I have spoken to only one person more than once (other than an immediate relative, mental health professional, or more recently, through asynchronous text chat online). Adding all those I spoke to only once would not increase the count substantially.

This, in itself, is an example of a maladaptation. People with AvPD generally still want, and need, social interaction for the same reasons anyone else does, and I am no exception, yet I avoid it completely for how terrible it makes me feel about myself. I am the type of person that would appreciate plenty of time alone anyway, but I am far past my limits in that regard. I sometimes have things I would like to do, if only I had other people to join me. Even if I did not, my anxiety is so severe that I've long been incapable of most forms of work. I realize that, to many people, that will sound like an excuse for laziness, but my anxiety is truly crippling to my ability to not only communicate, but even think about anything else, or even to complete tasks that require basic dexterity. Some people with less severe symptoms are able to work, as I hope to become, but their anxiety gnaws at them all the while, even in jobs requiring limited periods of interaction.

When I am absolutely forced to interact with someone, more maladaptations are made. Since I always think I'm making someone uncomfortable, I constantly hyper-analyze myself, trying to prevent or correct the mistakes that might cause this. Where are my hands and eyes? Is that hair on the back-right side of my head standing up again? What exact words should I say, with what inflection? Great job: I mispronounced that word, skipped a letter in the middle of the next one, said another in a heavy southern accent, and ended the sentence at an imperceptible volume—not to mention that what I said made literally no sense in the first place. There are truly an infinite number of minuscule things I'll worry about doing or having done.

In the same vein, I need to know when someone has noticed my mistakes, so I extend this hyper-analysis to them. If you raise your eyebrows a millimeter, cough into your hand for an instant, or slightly raise the pitch or volume of your voice, I'll notice it, and I'll probably associate it with some mistake I feel I've just made. It makes me feel horrible to notice these things, thinking I've made you uncomfortable, but I have to watch, so I know when it's time to find a way out. I don't want to continue making you uncomfortable, but more than that, I can't stand the possibility that you'll raise the issue outright. Right now, at least I don't know for sure that I really made you uncomfortable; if you mention something silly I did or said out loud, even in a way that's completely non-confrontational, even jokingly, there's no room left for that doubt—which only makes me feel even worse about myself.

Every type of social interaction, not just face-to-face, brings its own anxiety, and accompanying fixations and hyper-analysis. Asynchronous text chat like email, text messaging, or anything similar is by far the most manageable, but depending on whom I'm talking to, it might instill a great sense of dread. I'll proofread my message a hundred times, finally send it, then worry that I left something out or said something stupid, right up until the moment they reply. Live text chats are easier than some things, but they still cause me to panic, as I try to type as quickly, sensibly, and grammatically-correctly as I can.

Video calls emphasize the aspect of self-consciousness—I would worry about whether my camera quality is too terrible, whether I'm sitting too far from the microphone, how I look relative to the camera angle, whatever might be in the background, the lighting...and after all that, it still has all the challenges of an in-person interaction. Phone calls might seem that they'd be easier, since no one can see me, but they actually tend to be the worst for me. I can't find the signs of discomfort in people that I usually look for in their facial expressions and body language, so I have to live with an extreme fixation on their voice, heard through a low-quality microphone.

To be clear, this hyper-analysis is involuntary. I start doing it unconsciously as soon as I'm around anyone else, in any sense. Of course, I realize I've done it, but only after it's already caused a change in my behavior, which usually means fleeing from the situation. It's exhausting, and it only increases my anxiety. The intensity is variable, but it's always there. I realize how illogical it requires me to be: reading into minuscule signs that others make, usually unconscious and meaningless, to find evidence for what I expect— that they're uncomfortable with me.

Why, if I realize that it's illogical, can't I just stop doing it? That question really applies to all of my anxiety, which is based on assumptions that my brain makes, despite rarely having a particularly convincing reason at the present for doing so. There's a technology analogy I like to use to explain it: imagine you download a program for your computer, or an app for your phone, that's not from an official store. Maybe someone you know developed it, and asked you to test it. When you open it, there's a popup message, warning you that the app might not be safe to use. A fair warning, but one you believe in this case not to be true, and you can easily close the popup and continue. But what if there's a weird error with your device, and another popup appears? You close it, distracted for just a moment before you keep working. What if the popups just keep coming? It's like the more you close them, the more come back the next time. Eventually, the entire screen is covered. Yes, technically, you can keep closing the popups and try to use the application. But it's impossible to ignore them. Of course you can't use the application the way you're supposed to. More than likely, you just stop trying.

That's what it feels like to deal with social anxiety from AvPD. I know the things I'm so anxious about probably aren't logical concerns, but they just keep popping up in my brain whenever I try to interact with someone. They make it so nearly impossible that I give up. What caused this error in my brain in the first place? I think to some degree, it's genetic—I've been anxious of other people since as early as I can remember. As a four-year-old, I ran and hid to try to avoid going to school. As a seven-year old, I made myself vomit with the same goal.

But I don't think it would have developed into a personality disorder without the experiences I had. In short, there have been many times in my life (especially early on) where people took significant issue with my smallest faults, and far fewer experiences of being passionately praised for successes, or earnestly forgiven for mistakes. When I think something positively about myself, I doubt that it's true; I feel that I'm just being egotistical to think that of myself. When I reflect on my flaws, I feel a heavy guilt, feeling that I want to fix them, but also that they have felt so true, for so long, that it seems impossible; they are who I am. I have developed an expectation that other people will see me that way, and treat me accordingly; that it only makes sense, and that I deserve it. In the context of my past, my fears are plenty logical.

If you don't have AvPD, it might still be hard to understand why being criticized more than being praised affected me so deeply, where you might have shrugged it off. There is one theory about why that might be, which I find compelling. Some evidence suggests that people who, thanks to their genetics, have high *sensory processing sensitivity*—dubbed by psychologist Elaine Aron to be *highly sensitive persons* (HSPs)—react more emotionally to both positive and negative feedback. As someone who definitely identifies as an HSP (and has spoken to others with AvPD that do), I believe this is a major risk factor in the development of AvPD. The topic of HSPs is out of the scope of this book, but I highly recommend Elaine Aron's website (hsperson.com) if you're interested in learning more.

The feeling that everyone will rightly see us as bad, uninteresting, or worthless is why paranoia is also a common symptom of AvPD. Our expectation that people will dislike us, and our fixation on watching for signs to validate that expectation, is a form of social paranoia, as is the feeling that people are doing the reverse to us—watching for signs that we are deserving of their dislike, when the truth is that most people are not nearly as concerned with our tiny, typical, perceived missteps as we are. For some people with AvPD, the paranoia can also become more than that, extending to a distrust of others even as far as their physical safety is concerned, as well as more general situational or societal paranoias. This is why it's not rare for people with AvPD to also be diagnosed with paranoid personality disorder (PPD). In my case, I deal with some general paranoia, like feeling like I'm being watched when I'm alone in my home, or having to triple-check that I locked a door, then still not fully believing it. However, it is not constant enough nor debilitating enough to me to impact my life in the way that AvPD does, and thus does not warrant the additional PPD diagnosis.

At least for me, I also think AvPD interferes with memory function. My hyper-fixations leave little room in my brain for taking notes about things that aren't possible sources of embarrassment. In the short-term, this means that I often overlook things that seem impossible to miss. If I go outside to grab something out of my car, I look around everywhere to make sure no one is around. Then, when I come back inside, if you were to ask me about the temperature outside, I would usually have no idea. This can also cause the aforementioned paranoia, as my mind is elsewhere when I'm doing something like locking a door; thirty seconds later, I'll be uncertain whether I actually locked it, because I'm always distracted by other concerns. In the long-term, this sometimes extends to entire events or periods of time. If something made me extremely anxious, yet didn't result in an embarrassing experience to dwell on, I will often forget about it entirely within a few years. This became obvious to me when writing this book, when others reminded me of things that happened with me, which have almost completely faded from my mind.

Another symptom of AvPD, an extension of the social anxiety, is the panic attacks. My baseline level of social anxiety often triggers a handful of mannerisms— if you noticed them, you might think they were a bit weird, but you wouldn't necessarily correlate them with anxiety, or at least any more than average shyness: trying to look generally towards your face when you're speaking to me, but avoiding eye contact; often failing entirely, slouching and staring at the ground; making a strange face with lips pursed in a pseudo-smile, and eyebrows constantly raised; pacing, often back-and-forth in a very small area; putting my hands half-in, half-out of my pockets and drumming my fingers on my legs; or "drumming" my teeth together to a song in my head, which is visible as unnaturally fast back-and-forth jaw movement.

These anxious mannerisms are unconscious, but when I realize I'm doing them, I can stop them to some degree, with intense focus. Panic attacks, on the other hand, bring their own set of physical symptoms which are completely beyond my control, and make it that much more impossible to just ignore my anxiety. These happen for me when someone says something that makes me feel ashamed of myself, which can include criticizing me, or something I've done, but can also include simple confusion—if I ever have to clarify myself, I feel stupid for having not spoken clearly in the first place, but also might wonder whether they understood what I meant perfectly, and just thought it was a stupid thing to say. Sometimes, any question I'm asked about myself can induce a panic attack, even if it was clearly a matter of pure curiosity or interest in me —the person who asked might be judging me momentarily, when I answer, if what I say seems strange to them.

My panic attacks vary in severity, generally based on how long they last, and can happen while talking with anyone that I'm not, relatively speaking, extremely comfortable with (which currently includes only my best friend and my brother). The physical symptoms appear more or less in a set order as my panic intensifies. First, my already somewhat elevated heart rate skyrockets. I sweat an abnormal amount, sometimes from the forehead. My eyes tear up noticeably. Then, I get a stomachache, usually accompanied by a headache or dizziness, and occasionally by chest pain. Any worse than that, and the symptoms become extremely obvious to anyone looking at me—I have difficulty breathing, and start hyperventilating; my entire body shakes, most noticeable visibly in my arms, and audibly from my teeth chattering with the shaking of my jaws; my voice is shaky, and I stutter when trying to speak.

SELF-LOATHING

People with AvPD also dwell on any mistakes they made, or believe they made—or even feel they almost made—for far longer than is typical, or remotely beneficial. I might think about something stupid I said or did, feeling constantly ashamed of it, for a week or longer after it happens. During that time, I also recall the many other occasions I ashamed myself similarly, and feel it all over again—mentally and physically. It feels like receiving a permanent incapacitation every time I subject other people to my presence. The only question is exactly how bad it will be: if I am certain that another person (or multiple people) also noticed my source of shame—which I definitely will be if I have a severe panic attack—the pain will increase exponentially.

As such, I also dwell on non-specific similar mistakes I feel that I might make in the future. This generally disincentivizes me from participating in life, but also causes any scheduled social obligations to act as sources of dread—from the moment I know they will happen, until after they have concluded completely. For instance, at the time I am writing this, I have an appointment with a new psychiatrist scheduled for about two months out. Anything that brings my mind to doctors, or thinking about AvPD at all, reminds me of this appointment. The last psychiatrist I went to believed that he understood my issues completely; he made me feel stupid when I suggested that he didn't seem to understand me as well as he thought; he made me feel that my issues were a simple, almost laughable matter, and that if only I could be patient and continue to pay him, he would doubtlessly fix them completely. I thought he was incorrect, unfair, and maybe a bit pretentious, but I'll always harbor the doubt he made me feel. I want to try again, with another doctor, but I worry the same things will happen again. I feel disgusted at myself, wondering whether I'm too stubborn to get over it, or just too weak. My heart races and my chest aches just thinking about it.

In fact, this self-hating fixation over past shame means that I don't have to experience shame again, personally, for it to all come back. There's a fun phenomenon I call *secondhand shame*. If I witness an interaction, even between strangers, which results in someone's embarrassment, I feel their shame as well. This can happen even without obvious embarrassment, if I feel that I would have been embarrassed by the interaction, had I been involved. Really, this only *doesn't* happen if everyone involved is so immensely self-confident that they are able to project how unashamed they are onto me. As unbelievable as it might seem, this even applies to fictional entertainment. If a character in a book I'm reading does something embarrassing, I might cringe, turn red, and have to stop reading for a minute. I rarely watch TV shows at all, because most of them are absolutely agonizing to sit through. Episodic shows like sitcoms, that rely on character gaffes for their conflict, have me pausing constantly, and often giving up before making it through an episode. It's not that I can't see the humor, but rather that the emotion just feels too real, even when the actual scenario is completely unrelatable. I generally prefer absurdist humor for this reason.

Dread, panic, and shame—all these different, constant sources of anxiety have given me the expectation that there's always something to be anxious about. This expectation manifests itself as what I call *passive anxiety*: when I avoid everything completely, and have nothing to dread, nothing to remind me of shame, nothing to induce panic, and feel OK enough to completely immerse myself in palatable distractions—music, video games, fiction writing—I am still anxious. Sometimes less so, and not in any specific ways, but it's still there, in my head and chest, as if reminding me of the time passing—wasting away, as I try and fail to forget about the rest of humanity—while also serving as a warning of what awaits if I seek to rejoin it.

Sometimes, my brain tries to mitigate this passive anxiety with another maladaptation—maladaptive daydreaming, or "fantasization", as it's often called in the context of AvPD. For me, AvPD fantasies are a very specific sort of daydream, about something I wish I could do or experience. They always involve a dialogue between one other person and myself, though it's not really me—it's like a second-person version of me, that does everything the way I tell him to; the person I wish I was. Usually, these are triggered by something specific I'm doing or seeing. If I'm writing music, I might dream that I've recorded a complete album, and I'm being interviewed about it, imagining specific questions and compliments. If I'm watching something, maybe a YouTube video, and come across someone with an endearing personality, I might dream that I've met them in real life, and that they like me as well. These intrusive thoughts are very engrossing while they are occurring. I will snap out of them if something sensorily distracts me, but if I'm just sitting around alone, they occur very frequently, and I'm just along for the ride.

It might sound nice to have these thoughts take you over at random, and it kind of is. It distracts me with pleasant feelings for a time. But in the end, I can't help to consider—what would have happened if the real me was put in this scenario? I want to be the smart, funny, kind person I am in my imagination, but I am not him. No one would react to me in the way I imagine them reacting to the ideal version of myself. In fact, the real me has no way of ending up in these scenarios in the first place. He never leaves his house; he never shares the music he writes with anyone else; he never even speaks to anyone. I try to keep hope that I will become the person I want to be someday, but with AvPD, the path forward always seems to be in the opposite direction from the one I'm facing. And, given my low self-esteem, these fantasies also make me feel guilty, as if I'm being narcissistic to imagine myself being successful at something, or happy with someone.

Some people with AvPD also have intense attachments and anxiety of abandonment. This includes the feeling that they cannot emotionally survive without those closest to them, and a fear that those closest to them are likely to abandon them because of their flaws. They may often seek assurance from those people that this isn't the case. This is also a symptom of dependent personality disorder (DPD), and as mentioned earlier, it's not uncommon for people to be diagnosed with both AvPD and DPD. I don't relate as much to this symptom, but I will not be surprised if it arises in the future—as of yet, I'm not sure I've had anyone in my life that I might have developed such an attachment to.

As a result of all of these sources of anxiety, most people with AvPD also suffer from depression. Personally, I have also been diagnosed with persistent depressive disorder. My depression is deeply interrelated with my anxiety—another wonderful feedback loop—and I will talk about it throughout my story. I think most people are familiar enough with depression that I don't need to give a deep explanation at this point. It feels like being chained above a bottomless pit, feeling unable to do anything; having no choice but to stare into darkness, terrified of the prospect of falling in; yet, feeling that if you did, the only thing that would change is that your fruitless suffering would end.

When I am particularly depressed, I (and some others with AvPD) also experience a third type of fantasization—that of my own death. While I deal with suicidal ideation almost constantly, this is a specific type of it that works its way into my daydreams. I'll imagine that I've died naturally, and that two people are talking about me to each other, lamenting my passing. Sometimes I imagine that I've failed a suicide attempt, and someone is sitting in the hospital by my unconscious body, crying as they're saying words I can't hear, about how much I mean to them.

Sometimes, I'll imagine that I've succeeded, and someone is reading the note I've left for them, finally realizing that I wasn't making excuses, and that I wasn't exaggerating, and that I just wanted them to care. These thoughts never make me feel better, always worse, but when they come, I have to watch them. It's as if my brain is trying to remind me that I might be too lost right now to know how much people care about me, but that they do, and that I have to just believe that.

DISPOSITION

I've mostly focused on symptoms until this point: the common elements of AvPD that directly cause its most crippling maladaptation, summarized in one word as *avoidance*. However, there are additional maladaptations I experience: these have a less direct effect on my inward avoidant tendencies, and a more direct effect on my outward personality, and therefore on the people that I do interact with.

In my experiences speaking with other people with AvPD, I have observed that while a great deal of the causes, symptoms, and maladaptations are often fairly consistent between us, any potential outward personality maladaptations vary much more widely. I point this out because I want to be completely open about how AvPD has affected me, personally, without creating or furthering any stigmas or stereotypes about people with AvPD, other personality disorders, or any other mental health issues.

One of these maladaptations I have personally had a hard time with is defaulting to sarcasm. I'm not a particularly good conversationalist for a variety of reasons, one of which is that I'm exceedingly uncomfortable with showing significant emotion in most settings. People tend to think that you don't care about what they are saying when you make very mild, forced facial expressions, speak constantly in a quiet, near-monotone voice, offer short sentences built from a small selection of passive vocabulary, and rarely so much as chuckle or sigh. I'm very empathetic, but very poor at conveying it with the earnest emotion people need.

Feeling trapped by anxiety and depression for so long has, at some times, left me feeling cynical, which means that sarcasm is a natural fit for me. It really can be a useful tool—even when my voice is dry, my words can carry the emotion in its stead, and I can show you that I'm paying attention to what you're saying. When you're annoyed at someone, I can show empathy by saying something sarcastic about them; when you're nervous about something that I know you'll do well, I can reassure you by sarcastically commenting on your knowledge or abilities; when you're bored, I can make you laugh in a hundred different ways.

Of course, there are also an infinite number of scenarios in which sarcasm is the wrong choice, of which I don't think I need to offer examples. We've all met a smartass who retorts to everything we say. Unfortunately, I've been that person sometimes. Even when I'm too anxious to offer my opinion or show my emotions, I still have what might euphemistically be called "dry wit". It's like my brain knows that if it stops long enough to think before I speak, I'll decide it's better to say almost nothing, and just wait for whoever I'm talking with to get tired of me and leave, so instead I throw out the first quip that comes to mind.

A similar maladaptation is a tendency towards self-deprecation. This comes even more naturally than sarcasm, thanks to my AvPD fixation on my own flaws. I'm extremely familiar with what I don't like about myself, why I don't like it, how persistent and horrible it is—and how much of it there is. If someone feels bad about something about themselves, I'd like to comfort them, but as I mentioned, I'm terrible at doing that. But chances are good that if you perceive some flaw in yourself, I've noticed something similar about myself. I can show that I'm listening and empathizing by shit-talking myself!

Even better, if I have any reason to believe someone might bring up a criticism of me or something I'm doing, I can beat them to the punch, and avoid some of the shame of being reassured of my flaws by someone else. Add in some signature sarcasm, and it's hard to tell if I'm joking or not. You might laugh—easing my anxiety a bit—while also feeling like you don't need to make a criticism yourself, since I might already have some sort of awareness about whatever I messed up.

Of course, constant self-deprecation comes with a couple obvious downsides. It doesn't particularly make sense to try to reassure someone worried about their own flaws by essentially saying "yeah, same". It's probably more likely to make them feel worse in general, rather than relatively better about themselves. When someone responds that way to you, it probably seems like they're responding to the words you're saying, without really responding to the person saying them. And of course, if you can't appreciate yourself, other people will probably have a hard time discovering what they might appreciate about you.

There's one more maladaptation I want to mention, but it's a bit too specific to give it a name. When I am interacting with most anyone, I tend to timidly accept any judgment or criticism, whether perceived or explicit, without standing up for myself whatsoever. Take a high school group project as an example. If someone else in the group questions a bit of information I wrote down, politely and earnestly, I will probably tear up in embarrassment, mutter a vague response and withdraw the information. I will hope no one brings it up again, and bury the feeling that I deserve to offer a real answer, because I want to avoid a conflict that would probably embarrass me further. Even if someone vehemently criticizes me in a way that's untrue or unfair, I offer a similar non-response.

Most of the time, I'm anxious before anything has even happened. When I inevitably do something that someone else says is wrong, I think that they're probably right to feel that way. I was expecting to feel stupid and embarrassed, and now I do, so what exactly am I contesting, if I open my mouth to defend myself? Of course, that doesn't make sense, but that's how it feels in the moment. And yet, I'm not actually apathetic about being a timid person. If I feel that I am correct about, or justified in something I say, I want my belief to be understood—not to be right, or to be agreed with; just to feel like people know where I'm coming from. But, unable to speak up, I keep the defense I'd like to make for myself inside.

Around people I've known a long time, whom I should be able to trust, I'm more at ease. I'm not necessarily expecting to feel stupid and embarrassed. So imagine finally—rarely—feeling comfortable, and being shown that you were wrong to feel that way. To be called out by someone close, who knows how badly I already feel about myself, who knows that I'm trying really hard to keep trust in them—is an unimaginable feeling. I wouldn't want to describe it with a word that sounds as melodramatic as 'betrayal', but that word conveys the disgust it makes me feel in myself for having trusted, again. And, sometimes, when I feel this way, all those defenses of myself I've been too ashamed to make pour out at once. It's more than I really want to say right now, to this one person, but I spit it out anyway.

This collective experience is similar to what psychologist Theodore Millon described as the "hypersensitive" subtype of AvPD, but I think you can see why that name alone doesn't quite do justice to the experience: of feeling pathetically weak-willed in two alternating and antithetical ways; never able to defend myself with intelligence or thoughtfulness, only able to retaliate through despair. I hate both halves of this. I am determined to change them, and I think I finally have some idea how. But before I go into the future, I'd like to share with you my past.

FOSTERING MY NERVOUS NATURE

I was born in 1998, an early Gen Z and the middle child of an older sister and younger brother, in the southeastern United States. I have a lackluster recollection of my life before middle school, and virtually no memories from before kindergarten, as seems to be fairly typical thanks to childhood amnesia. Still, my mom's memories of me have always painted a believable picture.

It was the first morning that I would be attending preschool. I could meet all the other kids, and later, supposedly impress them with my ability to read "Go, Dog, Go!". Apparently, the prospect was not enticing to me. Mom let me out of the car, and made the mistake of being momentarily distracted by something else. I took off, running around the school grounds, looking for a place to hide. After leading them on a grand chase, I was finally cornered by my mom and the school staff, and made to submit to their demands. This was not a one-time occurrence: I attempted the same again many times during my time there, later trying to trick them by calmly entering the school, before fleeing down the hallways.

Mom sees it as a cute and funny story. Maybe it is, but it's also pretty eye-opening. At a time when the closest things I had to traits of a unique personality were my favorite picture books and colors, I was already showing signs of social anxiety. Seemingly, I didn't want to meet new people, and once I had already met them, I was still uncomfortable being around them. Acting like that at such a young age, with relatively few experiences to shape me, definitely hints at some genetic predisposition towards anxiety—though it's possible that experiences I don't remember had a greater impact than I know.

But even if I was anxious around other people, I didn't dislike them. From what I am told, I had no behavioral issues in actually interacting with other kids; in fact, I was naturally polite, and had no qualms about cooperating and sharing with others (even if that didn't always extend to my brother), as I had learned that these were the right ways to act.

With elementary school, I retired my flight-based approach of avoiding anxiety. My guess is that I was developing more awareness of myself and others, and realized they were doing the same. Running around the school was not only an ineffective strategy for avoiding these other people, but would, in fact, draw much more attention to me. For a time, I think I accepted that there was no good way of getting out of it. I settled into the low-pressure environment: the subject matter remained simple, and the interactions between students very surface-level, throughout the first couple of years.

In general, I remember feeling pretty happy in kindergarten. In first grade, I began to really develop some self-esteem. I had always liked words and numbers, and was constantly reading books, clocks, and speed limit signs. Now we were reading slightly more advanced books, learning basic math, and learning to write. I was pretty good at it, and enjoyed it all, especially since my terrible handwriting was seen as normal at this point, rather than unusually horrifying (you don't want to see how I grip a pencil on the rare occasion I'm denied a keyboard).

In particular, I remember an activity we could work on during downtime, in which we wrote ascending integers on a paper scroll of grids, which we could lengthen infinitely by taping more grids to the end. The purpose was to teach how the digits' places interacted as a number infinitely increased, and I found the concept fascinating for whatever reason. I was determined to have the most sequentially-written numbers of anyone in my class. I achieved this arbitrary goal by writing each number up to nearly (or perhaps over) ten thousand, during what most students treated as free time. I was very proud of myself.

Physical education, or P.E., was a somewhat different matter. I have never been inclined towards being a particularly active person—I would go outside, but was more interested in chilling with our pet dogs, or playing imaginary games, than running around or playing catch. Pretty much as soon as I started school, kids began to point out that I "ran weird". They weren't wrong—I have walked with my feet pointed significantly outwards for nearly all my life, resulting in a penguin-like gait, which is evidently very obvious whenever I go any faster than a stroll. For these reasons, I was extremely self-conscious in P.E., especially when required to run laps around the gym. I broke my own rule of not embarrassing myself, and practically begged the teachers to let me sit out when running was required. On at least one occasion, in response to their denial of this request, I planted my ass against a wall, stubbornly and tearfully refusing to participate, resulting in my parents being contacted. Nothing really came of that, as far as I remember.

There was no competition at school to the anxiety that P.E. caused me, but there was some at home. Looking back, it seems like my parents always treated parenting as a competition, each trying to prove to the other that their decisions were superior, and in that way prove to my siblings and I that they were the cooler parent. They cared about us, but they each cared at least as much about having things their way. Arguments would start over the smallest disagreements on raising or disciplining us kids, but would usually end with each parent personally attacking the other. My begging them to stop would generally have little effect, other than to fuel their annoyance towards each other, until I started to cry, and they felt some modicum of shame. I think a variety of factors caused them each to act this way.

Though they each, to this day, insist that they loved each other, I never saw any evidence of this, or any reason why it would be the case. My dad has trouble showing any emotion other than amusement or anger, has often been a habitual smartass, and focuses almost exclusively on working. He is fairly reluctant to spend money on non-necessities, except when it comes to his hobby of collecting endless gear and traveling for fishing and hunting trips—the near-singular hobby he has consistently had, since his age of four years. My mom is excessively emotional, hates sarcasm, likes spending money on random things, and loves relaxing and spending time with people. They seemed a truly terrible combination, and I can only assume were infatuated based on physical attraction. In any case, it is retrospectively unsurprising that the pair were prone not only to disagreements, but to quickly-escalating arguments.

Each also had conflicting views on family. My mom really wanted the stereotypical big, happy family experience: she would be the loving and caring mother, my siblings and I would be the mild-mannered objects of her affection, and dad would be the proud and stern-as-needed father. Reality did not allow for this scenario. Just because a person is your biological offspring does not guarantee that their personality will mesh perfectly with yours, which is a fact I don't believe my mom has accepted to this day. Though that presented more of a problem as I grew up, even early on Mom had a hard time dealing with the implicitly awful parts of raising toddlers—who are generally disagreeable, sometimes just for the fun of it. In her dream family, this is where Dad would step in.

In her real family, my dad was work-obsessed, and saw parenting mostly as my currently, voluntarily, stay-at-home mom's job, rather than a joint venture. His strategy towards raising kids seems to have largely been based around his own convenience. He thought we should be able to do most whatever we wanted, until something pissed him off, in which case we, obviously, should have never done it in the first place. Reasonably, his general apathy annoyed my mom. Less reasonably, she often handled it by presenting a small issue as a super-important problem with a huge disagreement between him and herself, as if getting him riled up was the way to force him to have an opinion, and defend it. It usually worked, causing him to angrily snap, and her to quickly reciprocate and escalate.

At this age, I only tended to be bothered by these parental arguments while they were in-progress, and they didn't come to mind while in class, or while hanging out with my new friends at school. I had "friends" before starting school, in the sense that I had hung out with a couple kids whose parents were hanging out with mine. But my school friends were the first ones I met independently of my parents. I have vague memories of these friendships at that age, but what always stands out when I think about them is how indifferent I was about the concept of friendship itself. I don't remember ever approaching anyone else, trying to start a conversation at lunch or recess. I wasn't anxious about it; it simply didn't occur to me to try that.

Apparently it did occur to others at that age, because I remember doing the things elementary school friends did: screwing around outside at the same places, with the same people; debating the quality of each other's lunches; one of my very first friends ended up being one of my best friends even into high school; but none of that was my idea. I think part of the reason

I didn't really try to make friends was the "stranger danger" sort of lessons my mom so anxiously imposed upon me; of course, she hadn't meant that I should be afraid of other kindergarteners, and I never believed that she did, but I think specific paranoid or disparaging ways she sometimes spoke about others contributed to some misgivings. Mostly, though, I just didn't feel an urge to make friends, and since I ended up with some anyway, no one really thought to explain to me the importance of things like being confident, and showing interest in others. Being a bit late on understanding the concept of making friends might not be that unusual, but I do think it contributed to insecurities that arose later.

Soon enough, second grade began, and things changed a little. Everything just became a bit more "real"—conversations were slightly less mundane, as kids' primary interests started to vary a bit; schoolwork was somewhat harder, requiring more effort and concentration than before. I remember one particular homework assignment I had—a set of math problems in a workbook. I solved them easily and turned it in. At the end of the week, I got my grade on it—my first 'C'. I got home and bawled my eyes out over having not gotten a perfect score and a smiley face. I had been told to do well in school, and now I had failed. My mom made some effort to console me, but, well, I had done the problems wrong, and my overreaction was getting irritating. I just needed to try harder and get it right next time.

I never really had as much difficulty with academics themselves as I did with insecurities over exactly how well I did. From the time I started kindergarten, my parents had taught me that the most important thing to focus on was to succeed in school. That's what would allow me to get a "good" job, which would make my life "easy" rather than "hard". Dad was a dentist, who ran his own business, and I could be, too, as long as I did well in school. Your level of success at school, and later with a career, is what governed how others would see you, and what opportunities you would have. This pressured me to never mess up at school—academically, but also behaviorally. My dad told me to "always be the bigger man". If you do make a mistake, own up to it immediately, and apologize. Better still, never make a mistake. If conflict was brewing, being the bigger man meant letting it go completely, no matter what.

My parents also got divorced around the same time. Soon began a shared custody schedule, which entailed spending half of each school week at one parent's house, half at the other, and alternating which parent's turn it was to "have" my siblings and I for a weekend. Relatively speaking, I might not have minded the back-and-forth driving, seeing pets at each house only half of the time, and having no idea where I left any of my stuff. After all, being subjected to fewer face-to-face shouting matches was pretty neat. Unfortunately, my parents were not going to give up their favorite part of being married that easily, and loud arguments over each other's personalities and parenting decisions moved to the phone. My tearful protestations were even less successful at calming them down than before, now that they were free to blame each other over the phone for how I felt, rather than feeling some degree of mutual embarrassment.

Fortunately, letting their rage reach the physical level was rare for my parents, though on a couple occasions, Mom flung expensive objects at hard surfaces, while screaming at whoever was nearby, and Dad pinned me or my brother to a wall by the neck, while angrily murmuring in our faces. Certain scary situations like these caused me, for a time, to seek comfort in calling the other parent on the phone, if they hadn't already been involved. Hearing my hysterics, that parent would relish the opportunity to comfort me, and then request to talk with the parent that was currently losing their shit. Another seemingly-endless argument would break out. The cycle would repeat in a few days, when us kids switched houses, and our parents reversed their roles. I eventually realized that I couldn't trust either of them, and I took to fleeing to my room alone, keeping my fear and sadness to myself.

Each parent made an initial effort to "be there" for us after the divorce—to talk things through, or just hang out—but after a while, each was too consumed in their own anger to want to spend much extra time with us, or think about us, beyond what they felt they had to. Usually, after that, if I wanted to spend time with them, I would have to agree to do whatever they wanted to do. For my dad, this meant going fishing or hunting with him, since these were his main interests for the majority of his life.

I came to hate both almost immediately—I didn't like to spend a ton of time outside, much less in the woods or on the water; I'm not a naturally patient person; and I didn't have the strength or dexterity to handle a gun or a fishing rod. Most importantly, I'm not the sort of person that gets joy out of killing animals, and Dad's remarks about *deer population management* and *fish not feeling pain* did little to change that. But those were the only times he really seemed to notice me, individually: when I was doing what he thought was fun and valuable. I tried to do both for some time, knowing he wouldn't notice, or care, that I was anxious, uncomfortable, and hating every second of it; just waiting for the moments he might look into my eyes without rage in his own; hoping that if I did well enough for him, he might congratulate or compliment me with some actual enthusiasm; thinking that maybe, eventually, he'd take a turn making a real effort to care about the things I liked.

Hanging out with my mom tended to mean family outings—movies, or bowling, or whatever else. I guess she loved the feeling of having a big day planned; it seemed like the only way that she could feel like part of her own family. I knew it could make her happy, and might remind her that we were still here. The events themselves didn't cause me particular anxiety at that point, but I was always a bit on edge, knowing that if anything went wrong, my younger brother might get upset, my mom would have a very hard time concealing her anger, and my dad—though separated from my mom—would somehow end up involved. Sometimes, it was because she'd call him to rant, blaming him for whatever had gone on. Sometimes, it was because she had invited him to come with us, and he had accepted. As they insisted then (and still do now), the two were making an effort—for us kids—to still "feel like a family". Obviously, that didn't work, but I don't think they ever cared about that. I think they were just so angry about their own lives falling apart that they were trying to make it work, for each other, and "the kids" were just a useful vessel to attempt that through.

The stress and anxiety caused by the divorce would only increase over time, but it didn't take long for my parents' constant rage to affect me. I began to develop physical maladaptations to try to keep myself calm and quiet during the distress. I chewed my thumbnails so hard and so long that I left tooth indentations in the centers of them, which took a long time to heal, even after I had stopped for good. I would wind strands of my hair around my right pointer finger before wrenching it out of my scalp, leaving bald spots on the top of my head, hoping no one at school would notice. I still find myself reaching to do that sometimes these days, but I keep my hair very short now, and consequently, I realize what I'm doing before I can get a grip on it. In spite of my stress and accompanying behaviors, for the most part, elementary school proceeded like second grade—having friends, but not thinking to try and make any new ones; generally doing well academically, but feeling disproportionately stupid and ashamed on the occasions that I didn't.

Around third grade, I was introduced to a new source of anxiety—crushes. Not that I actually had a crush on someone at this point, or that any of my friends did, as far as I know; rather, my sister decided that I did, or at least that it would be funny to tease me about a particular girl in my grade. Maybe it was just our usual kid sibling rivalry, or maybe she actually believed it. She liked to bring it up at dinner; as I indignantly and embarrassedly denied the accusation that I "liked" the girl, as most prepubescent boys would, my mom would laugh, then chime in and tell me that "it's okay to like girls!"

Such a statement might have been reassuring in the event that I actually did "like" someone, particularly if I had chosen to share that. In the context, especially given my age and subconscious apathy to socialization, it only fueled the embarrassment. I had gone along with the typical kid attitude, at least at the time, that boys were friends with boys, and vice versa. Though I wasn't uncomfortable around girls, and didn't dislike them, I wasn't even friends with one. I didn't have much idea what it meant to "like" someone in that sense—just enough to know that I definitely didn't. I began to experience discomfort when around this particular girl, just thinking about what my sister and mom had said. Fortunately, the anxiety didn't go beyond this mildly apprehensive confusion, likely because the thoughts were so far from my reality as the eight-year-old I was.

A preexisting, but intensifying source of anxiety at the time was my rhotacism. You may not have heard the name, but you're probably familiar: it's a speech impediment in which 'r' sounds are unable to be clearly articulated, and sound more like 'w'. The problem was not a new one for me, but more kids took notice of it, and liked to point it out amusedly. I began speech therapy classes at my school. I always felt embarrassed when I had to get up and leave my usual class, to go work on an element of pronunciation that most kids hadn't had any trouble with. These classes, and this embarrassment for me, had to continue throughout elementary school. Fortunately, they would eventually succeed in eliminating my speech impediment.

P.E. was also made more terrifying around this

time, as my grade began doing the "Presidential Fitness Test" twice a year, which was a poorly designed fitness program that American schools implemented until around 2013. All kids were required to participate in a series of challenges which they had not practiced for, or been educated on the potential usefulness of. They were then scored, compared to each other, and to the rest of the nation. It included curl-ups, push-ups, pull-ups, sit-and-reach stretching, a short sprint, and a one-mile run. In short, it felt like a way to figure out which kids would start playing team sports in middle school, and to embarrass everyone else. It was supposed to incentivize us to try to get fit, but the poorly explained and executed gauntlet format generally caused those of us who knew we'd do poorly to instead not try at all, so at least there'd be less for the others to laugh at.

I knew why those people were laughing at me. They really were so much better at fitness exercises than I was. But I also knew I was better than them at some things. I always finished my classwork faster; I spent my free time using my imagination rather than a pull-up bar; and, perhaps most importantly, I didn't laugh at people who were struggling. I wish that I had coolly walked up to them, and said something of that sort. But my dad had made it clear: being the bigger man meant not letting yourself get, at all, involved in conflicts, regardless of the words or actions of others towards you. So I said nothing, just listening to the laughter, and supposing that it would be enough just to think those good things about myself.

Third grade was also when my anxiety really started to manifest physically. If something had happened recently that had embarrassed me, or I foresaw such an encounter coming up, I would start to feel extremely sick to my stomach, from the moment I woke up. I began to avoid eating much, if anything, for breakfast, as it did not sit well if I was even a bit anxious. Many times, I wished I could just run away and avoid going to school, like I had attempted as a preschooler. At some point, it occurred to me that if I was really sick, then I wouldn't be able to go. If I already had a stomach ache, perhaps I was going to vomit, anyway. Maybe if I just hurried it along, I wouldn't have to go to school in the first place, as it wouldn't really be a lie to claim to my parents that I was sick, right?

So, on days when I felt especially anxious during the next couple of years, I deliberately gagged myself until vomiting, and successfully avoided going to school. My dad quickly guessed what was happening, but my mom always took my word that I was actually sick, which in a sense was completely true. It was not fun, to say the least, and I quit doing it of my own accord—in what was a relatively short time frame, considering that the anxiety did little to abate.

But around this time, I also have my earliest memory of my best friend, the only one I still speak to semi-regularly. I don't think it was the first time we had spoken, and I'm not sure that we talked a ton immediately afterwards, but for some reason it's how my brain remembers becoming his friend. The third- and fifth-graders were currently spending their recess time engaged in a war between each other, and the younger group was laying siege to the "fort" in which the older kids holed up every day. My friend—I'll call him James, in lieu of his real name—had brought a pizza delivery box, and explained to me that he intended to use it as a shield. It's such a small and specific memory, and it's a bit peripheral to my story for now, but it's something that sticks out in my mind when thinking about third grade.

In fourth grade, I began what my school called the PACE program. If you consistently (and accurately) finished your class work early, you could take a test to join, with parental permission. The idea was to continue engaging your brain in a different classroom, so you didn't distract other students instead. I was more comfortable just being with my class, but my sister had already been in the program, so when my parents received my "invitation" to take the test, it was expected that I do it. It ended up being more interesting than I had expected—rather than extra (or more difficult) work, it included a bunch of activities about "learning how to learn"—logical thinking and such. I developed a bit of confidence in my intelligence in doing this, which I don't think I would have otherwise.

Fifth grade was more of the same. I was pretty comfortable by then, as far as school was concerned, being in the oldest age group in the school (though myself a year younger than most), and soon enough it was over. However, I had also gotten old enough by now that I was beginning to feel the impact of my parents' anger more viscerally. As a little kid, it made me feel sad and scared. As an eleven year-old, I felt more anger, guilt, and heart-pounding stress—unsure if it was my fault, or why I deserved it, or what I could do to make it stop—and it gradually became more of a distraction.

Throughout elementary school, my interests

changed very little, and there was very little to them. I mostly listened to whatever music my parents chose on the car radio, mostly 70s and 80s rock, occasionally contemporary pop. I spent my free time with my brother, playing inside with toys, or outside with pet dogs, or watching whatever cartoon the TV landed on. My mom, having very specific ideas of what things it was alright for us to learn about or enjoy, had always been strict about our use of the family computer, particularly in any video games we might want to play. My dad, on the other hand, really didn't care at all. My brother and I respected Mom's rules even when we weren't around her, but due to the nature of the internet, we'd stumble upon something cool, and then beg relentlessly for permission to keep looking at it.

During the summer break before I began middle school, Mom got sick of our constant nagging, and more or less gave in, and it was then that my own personal interests began to develop. As it turned out, there was music that was more energetic than AC/DC, and games that were more interesting than poorly-made bowling simulators. Even then, Mom made her thoughts about my interests well known, whether it was that role-playing games were evil and sacrilegious, or that metal music was, well, also evil, and more like noise than music, anyway.

This didn't stop me from doing the things I wanted to, as I knew I wasn't hurting anyone else by doing them, yet feelings of doubt and guilt began to form around them. Would people be uncomfortable around me, knowing what I liked? Did what I liked reflect badly on me as a person? I became very guarded about what I'd share with who, not trusting anyone to give my interests a fair chance, expecting that they'd just dislike me—perhaps passively, or often outwardly.

As summer came to an end, my new interests, and my increased awareness about my family and myself, would play a role in the definition of my personality as I began middle school. The comfort of being among the biggest kids at my old school was gone, replaced by an anxiety that was familiar from when I was just starting school, but with a new severity: imparted somewhat by the experiences I'd had since then, but also much from what it seemed that middle school was—or would mean to me.

AS AWKWARDNESS BECAME ANXIETY

My new school was not only unfamiliar to navigate, but was also much larger. There was also much more moving around to do: where elementary school assigned kids one teacher per grade, who would teach them and their classmates most or all subjects, middle school introduced a schedule of six daily classes—different teachers, different classrooms, and different classmates—which changed somewhat each semester. Kids from as many as four different elementary schools were funneled into this school, meaning that I had not yet met a majority of the people that would be in my classes. The classes themselves were more focused on implementing things you had learned, rather than just memorizing them. I was aware, and acutely anxious, of all of this, in the weeks and months leading up to the start of sixth grade.

The first day came, and in spite of every class period

being taken up entirely by teacher and curriculum introductions, there was plenty of anxiety to occupy me. During class downtime, most students would turn around at their desks constantly, looking curiously at all those adjacent to them, chatting with anyone they recognized, and everyone they'd never met. That left a handful of us, who mostly stared uneasily at our desks, responding uncertainly when spoken to. For the first time, it occurred to me that I was supposed to be making friends. In elementary school, my classmates were the same for the whole day, not to mention the whole year. One of them was bound to randomly start talking to me, and make it a habit. Gradually, I'd get more comfortable with them, and I could start being their friend back whenever I was ready.

Now, it was different: there were so many students, in so many different places throughout the day. With so many options, and less time spent around the same people, there was no guarantee that someone in any class, much less all six classes, would randomly decide to talk to me, and then keep at it when I responded halfheartedly. Everyone was developing their personality, and was getting better at picking up on other personalities that meshed with their own. If I was uncomfortable when someone spoke to me, they'd feel it too, and they wouldn't have any reason to push the conversation forward.

It was really uncomfortable just sitting there, listening to everyone else talk to each other, feeling their eyes glance at my anxiously hunched-over self, as they wondered why I'd barely respond to anyone. I wanted to answer someone, to make a friend, but how was I supposed to talk to someone I barely knew anything about? All these other people were doing it, but it didn't make any sense to me. I had new interests I would have liked to talk about with people that shared them, like heavy music and role-playing games. But I didn't want to chance bringing them up with someone who didn't like them—they would think I was weird, and make sure I and everyone else knew it. It would be easier to wait, to passively learn some things about everyone. But that wasn't really going to work. Most people were so much faster than me: they picked friends that made good first impressions, and they noted the weird kids that wouldn't be worth talking to. It's certainly possible to overcome such apprehensions, but it's generally an uphill battle, especially for the sort of person that gives that type of impression in the first place.

Back then, it felt like everyone was so aware of every mistake I made. With hindsight, I realize that my classmates and I were really just beginning to develop that kind of awareness. I wish I had realized how relatively painless it would have been to just talk to them. Back then, I loved myself—I felt smart, ambitious, kind, and happy. I wish I had somehow known how much easier it would have been to overcome my fear of others, before it grew into a fear of myself.

But we learn, foremost, through what we experience. In sixth grade, I experienced intense anxiety through a swathe of new experiences for which I felt entirely unprepared, and I learned which behaviors would help me avoid these experiences. Trying to make friends is the simplest example of the many I'll mention. Most people seem to have an instinct to make friends; they may not know the best way to go about it, but they have little problem figuring it out, through trial and error, during their days as carefree children. Though I did like to talk to people, I didn't have that instinct to seek interaction on my own terms. I only realized that I would need to do it when faced with the prospect of being uncomfortable and alone. I had learned how to act kind, thoughtful, and considerate, but no one had ever thought to teach me how to convey interest, empathy, or emotion—and I had been frequently discouraged from my natural attempts at doing so: through apathetic discomfort from my dad, high-strung concern from my mom, or anger from either one. Now, among a group of increasingly conscious and critical preteens, I would have to learn how for the first time.

Or, perhaps, I would learn instead that, among all the new stressors thrown into my life simultaneously, this stress could actually be mitigated by simply accepting whatever social status others assigned me. Feeling left out and conspicuous would still cause me anxiety, but seemingly less than if I attempted to fit in. And don't get me wrong—I did try. I didn't have a choice, in those very first few days, when everyone was so new to everyone else; nor did I the next semester, when I ended up in new classes, with yet more new people. I could go through my yearbook and recall some of the specific conversations I awkwardly attempted to have, with so many individual people, each of whom I would almost never speak to again. But I quickly learned to avoid it when I could, through a sort of negative reinforcement—people's uncomfortable reactions to my awkwardness felt like a punishment for attempting to change my behavior, and in that way incentivized me to keep avoiding them.

I remember one occasion distinctly—I had ended up at lunch with a group of people that I mostly knew very little about. They were talking about what they had done over the summer, and at one point, the conversation turned to video games. I listened with interest, but still didn't feel comfortable saying something.

At some point, someone brought up a game I had just started playing over the summer, and I finally decided to chime in and mention that. One guy laughed, and said that he had just *stopped* playing it, as it was a kids' game. Everyone else chuckled, and I turned red. The conversation turned to something else. Of course, what he said was stupid on multiple levels— the least of which being that the main demographic of that game is in their 20s or 30s—and I was pretty sure about that, even then. But that didn't matter to me. I wasn't quick or witty enough for a retort. I wasn't confident enough in my own interests to either defend them, or just shrug it off; maybe my mom was right, and I should just focus on "normal" things that everybody liked. And I wasn't socially inclined or skilled enough to fake my confidence; to just chime in again, maybe getting a better response this time.

But my budding social anxiety, though itself negative, was also reinforced in strangely positive ways. I had some classes with a couple of my best friends from elementary school, including James, and the surge of comfort I felt then showed me that I could manage without meeting anyone new. Yet, as luck would have it, there were still new people that would insist on having me as a friend, in spite of myself offering them no reason to do so.

During the first week, if not the very first day, a boy in my math class twisted around in his chair and made a random joke. I can't remember if it was specifically to me, or generally to whoever was in that area, and I have no idea what the joke was, but I smirked and chortled—awkwardly, but earnestly. That was all it took, and apparently I had a new friend—we'll call him Wes.

Wes was in more than one of my classes. He always wanted to make people laugh, and seemed to always know exactly what would do it for any particular person, at any moment. On the rare occasion that he failed, rather than feel uncomfortable and give up, he would persist more vigorously until he found an angle. It was also impossible for anyone else to make Wes feel uncomfortable, at least in a way he couldn't turn into something funny. When I was around him, I never had to contribute to conversations much at all, and when I decided to, I didn't feel very self-conscious about whether what I had to say was interesting, relatable, or funny, because he'd turn anything into something entertaining. I'd end up hanging out with a whole group of people at times like lunch, most of us not exactly friends with each other individually, but comfortable because of Wes.

Listening to him was not only comfortable, but enjoyable. Talking to new people was neither of those things. I was happiest at the time by hanging out with Wes, James, and other old friends when I could, and anxiously keeping to myself when they weren't around. At the time, it was as if I hoped that I would just magically get my social skills someday, and then I could start making new friends. In reality, I was giving up the best opportunity I had to develop those skills. Of course, whether or not I tried to make new friends was not a decision made in a vacuum, or really a conscious decision at all. How could I choose to take on more anxiety by talking to new people, when I was already overwhelmed by so many new sources of self-consciousness?

Most of the things I was suddenly self-conscious about are typical for sixth-graders; it was the context of my underdeveloped social skills, and lack of support at home, that I believe made the situation different for me. For example, I had started to worry about my weight. Though I was only slightly overweight, I worried that my chubby face and midsection were becoming obvious. This concern was validated one day when Wes made a fat joke about me during lunch. Though I don't remember the joke exactly, it was a pretty tame jab, especially coming from a middle school boy. Of course, at the time, it made me feel terrible; I tried, with only some success, to hold back tears. Wes apologized within half an hour—he hadn't meant to make me feel bad. In retrospect, it's obvious he just had a joke in mind and was looking for any way to use it: there were heavier people in our group whom he could have used it on, if he just wanted to be mean, which he didn't. He thought I would take it well, and everyone could have a laugh.

Unfortunately, only the latter half of that ended up being true. I started thinking about it a lot, especially during P.E. classes, which were a fresh hell in middle school. Forget twice-annual fitness competitions—now most everything was competitive, and the kids that were getting into sports loved to show off and shit-talk. I was never athletic, and never had any interest in, or knowledge of, team sports, and now I was specifically out-of-shape. Though I was not really singled out and bullied more than any other unathletic kid, it certainly felt that way when being yelled at by a team captain who was already more familiar with shooting hoops than reading books. My worst P.E. experiences were still yet to come, but this was the peak of my body self-consciousness.

I attempted to lose weight on my own, but I had no idea what I was doing, and no real willpower to do it—after all, my goal was to prevent the negative outcome of my size being noticed, rather than to earn some positive outcome. My parents didn't really seem to realize that my relatively slight weight gain was bothering me. I was not comfortable bringing it up to either one of them, but particularly to my mom, who had always been effortlessly skinny (her own words). Eventually, I brought it up to my dad, who had been obese for at least a decade at this point. Unsurprisingly, I suppose, he smiled and told me it was nothing to worry about. I did, at least, learn that I could stop any jokes about my weight by being the first one to make them. Everyone could have a laugh, without anyone having to insult me, other than myself. Self-deprecation became a tool that I would use increasingly often to deflect judgment or criticism from myself.

Being mildly overweight was, of course, the least of my bodily concerns as a preteen. I had participated in a short puberty education course in fifth grade, so I was not caught completely off-guard when I began puberty later the same year. Given how prude my part of the country tends to be, I'm lucky I was taught anything at all, but there were nonetheless many things I did not have any idea to expect, or have the most remote theory on how to deal with, which caused extreme anxiety.

For the first two or three hours of middle school, I felt pretty neutrally about girls. Boys and girls talked to each other, without the weird aversion there'd been throughout most of elementary school, so I just went with it—not as far as doing so myself, but only because I wasn't talking to anyone new. Then I walked into third period, glanced around at all the new faces, and did a double take. The girl I saw made me suddenly feel what it was to "like" someone for the first time, though I didn't immediately realize that was what was happening. I hadn't had any reason to believe I would ever think a girl had a pretty face, or like how she had done her hair, or notice that she was wearing little earrings, but suddenly all of this came to mind at once.

For reasons I didn't understand, I couldn't stop looking back at her. She just stood out from everything else. I hoped I wasn't staring, and I would quickly look away whenever I thought she might notice, but even then I couldn't stop glancing back. I felt like I was being obsessive and creepy. Yes, I had heard that "it's OK to like girls", but I didn't have any idea what that really meant. I had assumed it meant I might like them in essentially the same way I liked my other friends. It couldn't possibly mean that just looking at someone would make my heart race and my stomach hurt, right? Staring at her definitely wouldn't be polite, but what was I supposed to do with these feelings when they wouldn't go away?

I gradually started to develop unease when looking

at, speaking to, or getting anywhere near any girls—not because I had any problem with them, but because I felt like I would make them uncomfortable. I wish I had talked to someone about how I felt, but I didn't know who could help me. It would be too embarrassing to ask my mom about it, even if she hadn't already laughed at me when my sister had teased me before. My dad didn't seem to be capable of emotions other than anger and amusement, and he didn't even handle those well. In general, my parents had never given me a sign that it was OK to ask them questions about subjects like this. Rather, they had given me the impression that I would just know what I needed to know, right when I was old enough to need to know it.

I would describe myself, before this point, as simply having been socially awkward. Mostly because of coincidence and unconscious tendencies, I hadn't developed a full suite of social skills, and now, going into middle school, I was suddenly becoming very aware of that. Being in that situation at that age is not especially uncommon; I was not particularly more worried about what others thought of me than anyone else was. Yet, my reaction to my first crush may have marked the start of something more than social awkwardness.

It is, of course, completely natural to be attracted to others, to be increasingly self-conscious around those you are attracted to, and to be confused about where these new feelings are coming from. Most people eventually learn, through a combination of instinct and guidance, that the correct way to handle these feelings is to simply talk to the people you feel this way about: to get to know them like you would anyone else, to eventually tell them how you feel about them, in the least embarrassing manner someone of your age can manage, and to realize, if you don't both feel the same way, that you will find those feelings with someone else. People of varying personalities and social abilities will run into different obstacles in this process, and will lose —and gain—confidence through trial and error. I don't mean to suggest that most kids of middle school age have a complete understanding of these concepts, but they need to be thinking about them.

As it happened, I did not know how to get to know anyone. Though I had a fair understanding of my own emotions, I did not have any idea how to express them. And the only thing I knew about reconciling conflicting emotions was that anger didn't solve anything, and yet was a common response, for some reason. These issues alone were still just social awkwardness. If I had wanted to start working past this—to learn to make friends; to learn how to relate with people, and how they could relate to me; to feel good about sharing my affection—in spite of being a bit behind the curve, I could have tried, and there's no reason to believe I wouldn't have slowly succeeded.

Truthfully, I really did want to—but at the time, I didn't realize that. I knew the importance of being a good person: I was polite, kind, concerned, and unselfish, just as my parents had taught me. When people chose to talk to me, I was glad to show that side of myself to them, even if in an awkward and emotionally-limited manner. It was not what my parents taught me that caused my anxiety—it was what they did not. I knew what it was to be good, but I did not know what it was to *feel* good.

I didn't understand that it was alright to talk to someone just because I wanted to; that seemed imposing, inconsiderate, and selfish, when that might not be what they wanted. I didn't think that I could share any of my thoughts and feelings with them, when they might feel differently, and become uncomfortable or angry with me. I didn't know that there were ways that we could healthily talk about those differences in emotion, and it wouldn't be such a big deal. I didn't appreciate that I needed to take those kinds of risks with new people, to even have the opportunity to show my good side to others. I didn't even consider the possibility that, if I had talked to that girl I liked, she might have appreciated it, whether she felt the same way I did or not.

I didn't realize that, sometimes, I was supposed to think of myself, and not just everyone else. I didn't know that I wanted to try to make friends and show affection, because where other people were involved, what I wanted did not cross my mind. I was so concerned about making others uncomfortable that I kept all the discomfort inside myself. In my opinion, this is the point at which my amorphous social awkwardness took on the shape of social anxiety. This was the first major negative personality pattern I began to develop, and is one that is core to the existence of avoidant personality disorder. Though this would continue to affect me long after sixth grade, I would not consciously realize it until nearly a decade later.

The physical changes of my body only made all of this more terrifying. My voice was getting deeper, which was weird, but nothing compared to its constant cracking. I started getting taller, throwing my poor balance off further. Acne started, and along with it, the new anxious habit of scratching myself until I bled. Normal preteen sexual function began, and like most kids in my region, I had virtually no idea what was going on, and had to uncomfortably figure it out as it happened.

Sixth grade taught me that I hate unpredictability. A major new element of middle school classes was being called on by the teacher to answer a question. Most people aren't huge fans of being put on the spot, particularly since some teachers seem to revel in their students' humiliation, picking out the quiet kids and sending them to write their answers on the boards, and I was far from an exception. My intensifying social anxiety meant that I couldn't stand to be the center of one person's attention, let alone the judge and jury that were the teacher and the entire class.

I did well on assignments where I was given time and space to think—which meant that, when no one would volunteer an answer, I was among the people most frequently called on. Almost every time, I made some sort of obvious mistake, feeling distracted and rushed by everyone staring at me. Teachers seemed to love that, because I was so nearly right that they wouldn't have to have someone else try from the beginning, and they could use the opportunity to correct a common error. It was so embarrassing—to have a mistake corrected that I knew I wouldn't have made, if I was answering the question in a comfortable environment. I began to hate being in particular classes which I wouldn't have minded otherwise, constantly distracted by the stressful likelihood that, at any moment, it would happen again.

I also discovered that, almost paradoxically, knowing about stressful situations ahead of time was at least equally horrible, just in a different way. Most classes began to include presentations, where each individual student (or sometimes groups) would prepare a project over a relatively long term, and then explain it to the class. I liked that these offered me a chance to plan exactly what I would say ahead of time, and slightly reduce the likelihood that I would look like an idiot, as compared to answering a teacher's question at random.

I hated everything else about them. There was still plenty of chance that, with all the planning in the world, I would get tongue-tied, or forget something, or whatever else. Being called on meant, at worst, that I would walk up and stare blankly at the board like a moron for a minute, before writing something nonsensical, which, to be fair, was plenty bad enough. Presentations entailed at least five minutes of looking out at the class, trying to make eye contact, trying not to be self-conscious of my appearance, all while trying to formulate complete sentences about whatever uninteresting subject I had to pretend to care about. If I did something stupid, the likelihood that people would remember it was much higher. We'd had time to prepare, and now it was time to present; everyone was listening (or, at least, it seemed that way), and what I said either made sense, or it didn't.

This is when I first began to realize that anxiety wasn't just tied to people, or places. It could weave itself into any memory, or any thought, no matter how tangentially related it might have been. If I knew a class presentation was coming up, I'd stress myself out trying to get it done, as close to perfectly as I could, as quickly as possible. Even then, I'd count down all the remaining days, unable to stop dwelling on the inevitable disaster; feeling sick every time I entered that classroom, and worse when the teacher reminded everyone that they should be working on it. If we got to choose when to present, was it better to get it over with early, or look at everyone else's first, and see if I needed to change something?

In spite of being as ready as I could be for the presentation, every one of those five minutes ruined weeks of my life. Unfortunately, that is not an exaggeration. They were the single worst part of my life at the time, and each one of them never seemed to end: long after all presentations were concluded, and they had slipped from everyone else's mind, I was still thinking about how weird everyone thought I was, for how awkwardly I had done. If I had gotten a bad grade, it would reinforce my negative thinking; yet, if I had gotten a good grade, I would assume that the teacher graded purely on the content, choosing to overlook my poor presentation skills and anxious mannerisms, which the other kids would still remember every time they saw me. This was the second AvPD-like personality pattern that I began to develop: dwelling incessantly on the possible past and future judgments that others might make, or might have made, about me.

I started to unconsciously think about my life in terms of what stressful situations were coming up—whether next class period, or next week. There was one that seemed bigger than all others: my first band concert. Going into middle school, my parents told me that I should find an extracurricular to participate in.

My sister was going to be in chorus for the third year in a row. I was very much not interested in that, but I didn't have much idea what I was interested in.

Other than being terrible at a physical sport, concert band was pretty much the only option left for me. I did have some interest in playing music, and though my first preference would have been to play guitar, that was not an option offered at the school. I did like saxophone somewhat, mostly because of my mom listening to Kenny G, or my dad listening to Billy Joel, so I decided I'd give it a shot. I didn't realize at the time that I would be playing alto sax, which has neither the standout highs of the soprano, nor the smooth lows of the tenor, but that's beside the point.

Band class itself actually turned out to be pretty fun. Wes and one other friend were also playing saxophone, James and a couple other friends from elementary school were playing percussion, and there was often plenty of free time to do whatever. I did have to perform on an instrument I'd just started playing in front of a bunch of other people, but the fact that they were doing the same thing, at the same time, meant it generally wasn't so bad. However, there was a catch, in the form of one-on-one performance tests with the teacher. In spite of my band teacher being one of the nicest teachers I ever had, these tests were nearly as terrifying as class presentations, as every mistake I made in playing a scale, or any imperfection in my tone, was carefully noted. I turned out to be pretty decent, and was among the higher-chair saxophones in my grade (a ranking system which determined what level of complexity of part you'd play for your instrument), but that only seemed to increase my performance anxiety, as I wondered if I had set the bar higher than I could keep it.

Of course, I was also becoming increasingly aware of the fact that, by the end of the first semester, I was expected to play on a stage, for an actual audience. Yes, all of my classmates would still be playing at the same time; and yes, the audience would be composed almost entirely of parents and slightly-older band students. If I'd really thought about it, I might have realized that this concert was probably going to cause me less anxiety, while it was happening, than any one of my class presentations did—and in some ways, I did worry about it less, at any one time, than those presentations. Still, whenever I didn't have something more immediate to worry over, the concert always loomed in the distance.

Outside of school, my parents' tempers loomed as well. Separated, depressed, and angry after the divorce, each had begun to focus less on proving they were the cooler parent, and more on proving that our other parent was horrible. Over the intervening years, this tension had only increased. Distracted by feelings of their own lives falling apart, parenting wasn't the foremost thing on their minds.

They did care about us, and they put a lot of effort into a lot of things for us—working, cooking, cleaning, driving us around, helping with homework, taking care of pets; reading, playing games, or watching TV with all of us. At the same time, it feels like they went by a to-do list, thinking about the things they had to do for "the kids", more than actually thinking about us as individual people, before returning to their preoccupation with their failed marriage. If we were doing well at school, that was great, but more because it wasn't a problem for them than because of our achievement.

If, on the other hand, we had a problem with grades, attentiveness, behavior, or anything else, that was one more thing that they simply didn't have the bandwidth to think about. To that, their most frequent response was to get irritated at us, yell at the other parent over the phone to pass any blame onto them, and drink, with the objective of forgetting about it—not necessarily in that order. I was old enough now to be dragged, personally, into arguments between parents. I was expected to side with one of them over the other. There was nothing I could say that wouldn't get me yelled at or shunned, by one or both of them. Whenever I showed any emotion in these stressful situations I was forced into, I was reprimanded for being unreasonable, and told to calm down and shut up.

This side-taking in arguments caused increasing levels of paranoia in each of my parents, especially my mom. I think she had always had a tendency to read into things, but it became much more clear. The words I said, expressions I made, or interactions with my siblings I had were always questioned for negative intentions—even if I was being positive. A smile at my brother could mean that I was making fun of my mom. Anything I said might have meant to her that I liked Dad more than I liked her. She reacted very strongly to nearly everything that someone did, or what they didn't do: often actively, with strong words and intense emotion; sometimes passive-aggressively, just implying her distrust rather than stating it outright; and sometimes passively, as her mood silently changed with a moment's notice.

I felt guilty and embarrassed when something I did caused this reaction, rarely understanding exactly what I had done, but wanting so much not to have made her feel bad. I began to overthink everything I did or said, trying so hard not to ruin another evening for my family in this way; and I began to look for the subtle signs that I had done something wrong, so that I could try to calm and quiet things down as quickly as possible. Unconsciously, I began worrying about these small signs in others, and small mistakes in my own actions, no matter whom I was around. This would be the start of my AvPD hyperfixations, a maladaptation that intensifies my anxiety to this day.

While married, my parents had rarely attempted to work things out calmly and healthily between each other, but such a concept gradually ceased to exist for them entirely, regarding anyone close to them, once they had divorced. If talking to them about my various anxieties hadn't seemed daunting enough based on how I figured they'd react while in a good mood, imagine how terribly bad an idea it seemed to do so while they were constantly distracted and easily enraged. Instead, I would lie awake at night, cyclically, fruitlessly worrying, for many lonely hours in the darkness.

My parents did, on rare occasions, agree on specific elements of raising each of their kids individually. For sixth grade me, they felt they needed to make sure I started doing the same things my sister had when she began middle school. One example was trying an extracurricular activity; another was beginning to socialize with friends while outside of school. I was much more resistant to the latter: I was comfortable enough around my friends, but I was more comfortable doing what I wanted, on my own terms, during my free time. I could hang out with my brother if I wanted to play a game or joke around with someone.

Besides, I saw my friends all the time at school, where other kids, teachers, and classwork offered a constant stream of fresh conversational fodder to joke or complain about. I wasn't sure what would be left to talk about when that ran dry. I didn't see any point in going somewhere public to hang out, to do some random activity, and I wouldn't have been allowed to anyway. That pretty much left the possibility of inviting people to hang out at whichever parents' house I happened to be at on a given day.

I really had no interest in having friends over, or going to visit them if they had happened to invite me. But my sister had begun doing so frequently as soon as she started middle school, and my parents apparently decided that was typical, and perhaps even necessary. The possibility that my sister was naturally more sociable than I was didn't seem to occur to them, nor did they seem to wonder whether my disinclination towards socializing had any root in anxiety.

Their repeated reminders that I was allowed to have friends over eventually morphed into a sort of interrogation: why wasn't I inviting anyone? Was there some problem with our home or family? Are my friends bad people that make me uncomfortable? Eventually, partly because of exasperation, and partly because it had been hammered into me that it was "normal" to have friends over, I caved, and invited James, and another friend from elementary school whom we'll call Chris, to a Saturday sleepover. Both, being at least a bit more sociable than me, accepted.

There's not much to say about the resulting event, other than that it went exactly as I expected. We sat around awkwardly for a while, talking about things we had already talked about, then took turns playing a video game on my mom's laptop. My mom checked in a few times, seemingly confused that we hadn't retreated to my room to loudly gossip, as my sister often did with her friends. The time I usually went to sleep came and went, as I didn't have any idea how to tell my friends that I was tired and uncomfortable. Finally, morning came, and I relievedly bid them goodbye, resolving to never participate in such an event again. I couldn't imagine that I would ever like someone enough to hang out with them without planning a particular reason to do so. Though my parents did not stop reminding me that I could have friends over again at any time, they thankfully did tone it down a bit.

That was one of very few "major" events I remember from sixth grade, the main other being the long-foreboding band concert. I woke up that morning with the familiar stomach ache. It was nearly holiday break, and as such, the school day was extraordinarily uneventful. This came with the upside of not increasing my anxiety further, and the downside that there was virtually nothing to distract me other than Wes, who, for whatever reason, found it amusing to repeatedly ask me if I was ready and/or excited for the concert. Finally, I headed home to eat a snack and stew alone for a moment. I changed into my dress clothes, cummerbund and uncomfortable shoes included, all too aware of the fact that the tucked-in shirt did not lend the most flattering look to a chubby sixth-grader.

Shortly, it was time to head to the auditorium, in a county building near the middle school. The concert band would play first, which included the sixth graders and some older students, and we were then requested to hang around and watch the other bands—the symphonic band, which was the more advanced of the seventh and eighth graders, and the completely extracurricular jazz band. We had rehearsed on the stage before. At that time, I had walked to my seat alongside Wes, our usual joking echoing around the room, glancing out at the empty auditorium with only that distant anxiety. This time, as Wes continued to mutter joking remarks, I walked hastily and in silence, looking anywhere other than at the audience packed into the auditorium seating, my forehead glistening with anxious sweat under the stage lights.

The silence before we began was the worst part. I stared at my sheet music for what felt like forever, waiting on the percussionists to tune the timpanis or something. Finally, the band teacher counted us in, and a few songs and half an hour or so later, it was over. I booked it off the stage at the first opportunity, put my saxophone away, and breathed a sigh of relief. Wes and I found seats to watch the symphonic band, and from that point the only thing to be anxious about was Wes and I pissing off the people nearby by talking too loudly.

My parents loved it; or rather, my mom did, and my dad tried his best to convince me he cared, which was something. I appreciated their positive reaction very much, but I also took notice of where it seemed to come from: Mom just really liked saxophone, and had pushed me to choose it, specifically, when joining band class.

Seeing the difference between how she reacted to this, and other things I'd tried, and interests I chose on my own, made it feel more like she was praising the saxophone than I. Dad, of course, was not to be outdone by Mom, so he put a little more effort into his reaction than he would have otherwise; I had seen that before, from both of them.

While the concert was actually happening, it wasn't so bad. I even enjoyed it a little bit. Of course, as soon as band class resumed on the first day after holiday break, we started learning music for the end-of-the-year concert, and my anxious dread returned in spades. Though I didn't really recognize it at the time, this was the first sign of an illogical element to my anxiety. Other things that had caused me anxiety had been pretty well warranted, even if not to the degree that I was anxious about them, and even if I could have worked around them if I had known how. Though I wouldn't have expected to have been completely immune to performance anxiety after one short concert, the fact that I was even more anxious after having a smooth first experience suggests, with the context of my later experiences, that I had already begun to develop an aversion to anything that incurred risk of embarrassment—regardless of my experience in mitigating that risk, and regardless of any enjoyment I'd gotten from such experiences.

This aversion is core to AvPD. Once it surfaces, any bad experience will stack upon it, forever serving as evidence to its necessity: the necessity to avoid any possibility of becoming more ashamed of yourself. The only thing that can reduce it is to take a risk—and have it pay off. These past few years, I felt no deeper truth than that to take a risk was accepting permanent pain, for a small chance of temporary happiness. I have so little self-esteem left, even now, that each and every pain I feel makes me feel worthless, and disgusting; makes me wish that I could feel nothing. But back then, I still loved myself; back then, I felt an unconscious, lingering hesitation, but I still knew that I would go on. Maybe then, if someone had known exactly what I needed to hear, they could have gotten through to me— how so many risks presented such small downsides compared to the least of their upsides; how much I'd regret never taking any chances. Now, I know these things well; yet, after all these years of trying to feel safe, what I had in myself that I could have afforded to risk has almost faded to nothing.

Throughout sixth grade, all the new and changing sources of anxiety from socialization, classes, and home bled into each other—and yet, I was pretty happy. I ended up with new friends that formed my sense of humor and personality. I continued to do well academically, but also started to realize which subjects I really liked, or particularly hated. I enjoyed learning to play saxophone, and having something that I was good at, that not everybody knew how to do. And, in spite of how terrifying it was, it was kinda cool to have a crush on someone, though I never would have admitted it. For the first time, I was conscious of a sense of self. It was good to feel like I wasn't just some guy named Jake, but a specific sort of guy named Jake.

TRYING TO MEET EXPECTATIONS

Soon enough, the end of the year concert had gone by much like the first, classwork and tests were done with, and summer break arrived. My increasing obsession with video games had turned into a desire to make my own, and after a bit of fooling around with beginner development software, I realized I needed to learn a programming language. I asked for a C++ textbook for my birthday, and spent much of the summer learning the basics, and being half-jokingly called a nerd by my siblings. I also ended up with an electric guitar, and started learning to play the kinds of music I actually liked.

I did also make some effort to be more active, and as seventh grade approached, my chubbiness had begun to subside—but mostly because I was getting significantly taller, and my weight was naturally distributed more evenly. Maybe I would have one less source of anxiety. In fact, there was another less, as I would no longer be among the youngest people in my school. That had mattered to me more in sixth grade than in elementary school: not only were there more occasions on which students of different ages intermingled, but additionally, the differences between sixth and eighth graders were, in some ways, more stark than even those between kindergartners and fifth graders.

Of course, I knew that I would be plenty anxious getting started with new classes again. In seventh grade, this also came with the new experience of being called out by teachers that recognized my last name. As they called roll, reaching my name near the end of the alphabetical list, it seemed to be very important to quite a few of them to know if I was, in fact, my older sister's younger brother. When I confirmed their suspicions, they generally liked to remind me, in front of the class, how good of a student my sister was, informing me in a not-so-subtle manner that their expectations for my intelligence and behavior were starting at a high bar. That was a nice little touch on my anxiety, which would continue with new teachers from then on.

Band had concluded last year with more performance tests, and I had done well enough to be placed in symphonic band, which, though neat, was also nerve-wracking, as the music we were learning was suddenly much more difficult. For whatever reason—I think because of some combination of being asked to by the band teacher, older students, and Wes—I also decided to join jazz band. That meant that I would have to learn even more material, and also arrive at school forty-five minutes early a few days every week. I didn't particularly like jazz, but I guess I didn't particularly like symphonic music, either.

A week or so into classes, it did seem like I was going to be a bit less anxious that year. A bit more comfortable at the school, I even started messing around in class a bit, having learned the ways of not paying attention from my mentor, Wes. I ended up with another new friend, whom we'll call Isaac, again through no efforts of my own. We ended up randomly sitting next to each other in the back of our math class, and because of his sheer boredom and a slightly stronger social inclination than my own, he made awkward conversation about whatever he could think of, in an attempt to get me to respond with more than a few words or a nervous chuckle. Eventually, he mentioned that he played guitar, and I took the metaphorical bait. It didn't take long to annoy the teacher with our quiet but ceaseless conversation. As it turned out, he was the sort of teacher that threw Expo markers at kids who wouldn't shut up, and was also a former baseball pitcher. Fortunately, he didn't actually want to kill me, or I'm pretty sure he could have.

In that same class, I learned that I could develop a crush on someone I already knew. Maybe seeing this girl in a different setting is what allowed me to realize how much I liked her personality and mannerisms. Maybe my speaking more in class pointed to a lessening inhibition to feeling seen, which might have translated into less discomfort in paying attention to others. Either way, I still never spoke to her. Seeing how much a pleasant personality could mean to me only reinforced how much of an impact my own awkward mannerisms would have on others. I didn't consciously perceive it in that way at the time, but that sort of idea unconsciously guided my behavior. It was enough to appreciate seeing her be herself, without adding myself to the equation.

The year proceeded much the same as the one before it. Another two concerts went by, causing me similar anxiety as before. On one hand, I was a bit more confident overall—in my playing, my appearance, and in my general presence. On the other hand, the act of performing was no easier, and the parts I'd be playing were not only much more difficult, but also much more obvious when played incorrectly. Once again, the performances went smoothly, and yet each time, I still felt as terrified as the last. It is normal that people react to new experiences with trepidation, and sometimes fear; it's also typical that, each time such an experience goes poorly, you'll be less comfortable with trying something similar in the future. Inversely, if an experience goes well, you should be more comfortable with doing it again. Yet, even at a time when I was slowly becoming more comfortable with expressing myself, I seemed to only have the ability to get less comfortable with specific experiences.

Remove performance anxiety from the equation— no band concerts, presentations, or being called on in class—and there would still be a difference. What was it that kept from me the comfort to be myself and talk directly to new people, that didn't keep me from doing the same—if only a little—with my friends, while still around these same "new" people? With Wes, I might have just been getting carried up by his confidence. With someone like Isaac, the same could not be said— even if he was more inclined to put in the effort to make a new friend than I was, he would turn bright red at the slightest possibility of embarrassment, which was not the case even for myself.

I look back now at the decisions I made in middle school, as I discovered which types of situations were comfortable, which ones weren't, and which ones were worth avoiding at any cost. The common factors in my determinations were the expectations of others. What did I believe that the people around me expected from me at that moment? How much potential did I have to change those expectations? I thought about how many times people had assigned expectations to me that were too high, too nebulous, or just too different from what I wanted for myself. I thought about what happened when I failed to reach them. I also began to realize that, in some situations, I had been able to change the expectations that others would have for me.

Everyone sees patterns in the events in their life. Band concerts follow a very particular pattern, as do class presentations. When someone approaches you to make your acquaintance, the pattern is more subtle, but it's still there: you have expectations about the way in which they will greet you, the subjects they might talk about, the fun or relatable parts of their personality they might try to show, and what their goal might be in talking to you. These expectations change depending on the specific setting, but you almost always learn very quickly what to expect.

I was more comfortable in situations with less-specific expectations, but more than anything, I was comfortable when people weren't thinking about their expectations at all. If others are occupied with their own thoughts rather than their expectations of you, you make the choice of what expectations to bring to their mind. In sixth grade, I usually chose not to draw anyone's attention at all. By seventh grade, I had begun to learn ways in which I could express myself that would cause those around me to expect only what I knew I could fulfill.

Talking quietly, but frequently to Isaac during math class made me feel more normal. I had a friend whom I could share an interest with, and I could project the appearance of a natural, sociable kid. I chose to bring to mind the expectations associated with mild classroom distractions—namely, the expectation that I might cause a brief and amusing disruption in the lesson.

I felt a bit embarrassed when the teacher got annoyed and threw a marker at me, but I also didn't mind feeling like I had made the rest of the class laugh, breaking the monotony for a moment. If it left any lasting impression about me on someone, it would probably be that I didn't care that much about math, which would have conveniently served to lower their expectations for me in another situation. Messing around and talking to friends during class doesn't sound, on its face, like something that someone with social anxiety would do—and it certainly didn't remain something I would do, as my anxiety worsened. But at the time, it let me feel like I belonged.

In seventh grade, I was still open to trying things that made me anxious, if I thought they'd make me happy. More often than not, though, I tried them to make other people happy. When our band teacher invited us to participate in the "Rockathon" fundraiser —in which you would spend Friday evening through Saturday morning sitting in a rocking chair in the school cafeteria, in order to coerce your parents to donate to the band program—I reacted with amusement rather than my usual anxiety. There was literally no chance I would attend what amounted to a massive sleepover, in which participants were not allowed to move from their chair except to scoot it around a bit, or during predetermined bathroom breaks.

Spoiler alert: my friends, mostly Wes, begged me to come for days on end, and I caved—partially to make Wes shut up, and partially because I was trying to be a good friend, if he cared that much that I came. The regrettable experience that was my last (and only) attempt at having a sleepover still fresh on my mind, I reluctantly asked my parents, individually, to fill out the permission form. They reacted with predictably oblivious approval, as if I were suddenly now a social butterfly. All I could think about was how much worse it was going to be than my own small sleepover: trying to socialize with any number of people who I might barely know, before feigning sleep after everyone else had dozed off.

But it might have had a couple advantages: for one thing, between Wes and everyone else there, there wasn't going to be any awkward silence, at least until I was the only one left awake, unable to sleep around so many people. On top of that, the expectations were very different. A few friends hanging out at your home have fairly specific expectations of how you all might entertain, and be entertained by, each other. The Rockathon would be a lot more like free time in class—a lot of people that didn't necessarily know all that much about each other, shooting the shit until the bell rang—

with the key difference that this was our weekend being taken up, rather than class time. With any luck, everyone would be making an effort to entertain themselves, and I would have to contribute no more to a conversation than an occasional laugh on-cue.

The day arrived, and after classes, I had only a moment of respite at home before begrudgingly returning to the school. Everyone was setting up small circles of chairs, and I ended up in a group that was split, roughly evenly, between my friends, and people I had never personally spoken to. Unsurprisingly, most of them were friends with Wes, along with a couple percussionists that knew James and Chris.

It was quickly obvious that everyone else was going to be bored enough to constantly volunteer themselves conversationally, and all I would have to do was wait it out. One of the percussionists told a story about how he'd been medically dead for a few minutes as a child, and contended that this made him a vampire, which supposedly explained his pale skin. As the evening progressed, the conversation followed, entering typical middle school boy territory. The more socially-prolific half of the group talked about girls, while the rest of us awkwardly listened.

Eventually, I was roped into playing through the near-entirety of a Mad Libs book, along with mostly that other half of the group. One of the clarinet players caught onto the fact that I was rarely following the "plot" that was written, and after that, I received the sort of vocabulary lesson that was somewhat amusing, but mostly confusing and humiliating for myself as a sheltered twelve-year-old. When that finally ended, Chris and I listened to music on his iPod for a while, before most people either went to sleep, or pretended to, as I did, while the band teacher and parental volunteers continued to patrol around the room. Trying to sleep in that setting reminded me of the *Prisoner of Azkaban* movie, where the students are suddenly thrown into the Great Hall, and Dumbledore and Snape are just pacing around chatting, as if the people laying right next to them on the hard floor are as sound-asleep as could be.

Eventually, morning came, and I was left with just enough weekend to myself to dwell on school's inevitable return on Monday. The event hadn't been spectacularly horrible, but it had been uncomfortable, embarrassing, and more than anything, exhausting. Once again, something that was supposed to be natural and fun had been neither, for me, and I continued not to understand what I was missing that made me less normal.

The year was generally unremarkable otherwise, and then summer came around again; a couple of things stand out to me about the break. For one thing, my chores increased substantially. I had handled simple things like cleaning up after myself, folding and putting away my laundry, and taking out trash for a while. Now, each parent had more specific things they wanted me to help them with. I helped Mom with occasional house cleaning—mostly vacuuming, dusting, or window cleaning—and sometimes cooked dinner. With Dad, I did outside work, or "men's work" as he put it when explaining why my sister never had to help, which included things like mowing the lawn, as well as splitting and stacking firewood. As you might expect of a thirteen-year-old, I was not particularly thrilled with the prospect of spending my summer this way, and procrastinated plenty before getting around to chores.

My apathy was not my only reason for procrastinating. It turned out that I was not very good at most of these things I was now expected to help with. That doesn't seem very surprising, given that I hadn't really done them before, but my parents were not exactly the best or most patient teachers. Mom would look over something I had cleaned and roll her eyes, insisting that I had missed something very obvious. "Nevermind", she would say, when I asked her to show me my mistake, and would just redo the entire thing herself. When she occasionally gave me a second chance, still without explaining what specifically I had done wrong, the best I could expect was to hear that it was "good enough".

My dad, in spite of being overweight, spent a lot of time working outside and was very strong. Somehow, he expected a thirteen-year-old musician and computer nerd to replicate his results. I could barely pick up a maul or axe, much less swing it accurately at a piece of wood, and could not endure in the summer heat long enough to mow the lawn without frequent breaks, every one of which caught his attention, triggering a shake of the head, a roll of the eyes, or a rhetorical question as to how I had not yet gotten used to the sun. When I finally finished, he was too exasperated to offer thanks, preferring instead to point out how I could have finished it five times by now. He wasn't exactly wrong, but saying so was the opposite of either helpful or encouraging.

Occasionally making dinner felt, at first, like it might be different. As a kindergartener, I had thought I would want to be a professional chef as an adult, and while by now I knew that I certainly did not, I still enjoyed cooking, and thought I was decent at it, all things considered. Cooking a nice meal for everyone seemed like an easy way to make people happy, and maybe receive a compliment or two. When I was five, it had always turned out that way, in spite of what I cooked at that age being just on the threshold of edibility.

Now, I would make things that had room to actually be tasty, while still being simple, such as basic pasta dishes. Regardless, the reaction was lukewarm—my siblings didn't really care much either way, and I didn't expect them to, but I had hoped my mom would enjoy what I made. She did, she assured me—after asking what exactly it was, and why it didn't seem to have one particular spice that she thought should obviously be in something like that. It wasn't that she was mean, but that it seemed like she had missed the point, preferring to use the opportunity to display her own expertise in cooking, rather than just offer a compliment and save the advice for another occasion, perhaps when cooking along with me. I wasn't offended, just disappointed in myself.

While none of this really impacted my self-esteem at the time, I think it began to mentally condition me: to do my best, not to earn praise or thanks, but to avoid ridicule; and when possible, to avoid doing things, in the first place, that opened more opportunities for mistakes, however small. Whether chore-related, academic, or behavioral, my parents never tried to understand why I had made the mistakes I did, nor ever wanted to listen if I volunteered my own apologetic explanation. It was silly to ever hope for an apology for an overreaction, or for forgiveness for my own mistakes. All I could do was accept their criticism or punishment, and wait for them to forget.

My tendency towards risk-aversion had been an adaptation to avoid being ashamed of myself, out of a desire to feel that I was making the right choices for myself, and doing well at what I wanted to. Now, the reasoning began to shift: my concern over how I felt about myself seemed relatively insignificant, when compared to this increasing fear of how others felt about me. Negative thoughts that others developed about me would be relatively immutable, and while I would always have to be around myself, other people could always leave me. My thoughts began to turn away from what I liked about myself, because that meant nothing compared to what others disliked about me.

The other thing I remember about that summer was getting a bass guitar for my birthday. I had enjoyed learning to play guitar, but as I continued to pay more attention to the music I was listening to, I had realized that, not only did full-scale bass guitars look far more badass, but their low pitch offered a super-chunky tone to bands that didn't kill it in the mix. Listening to bands like Megadeth, I realized that bass could play a uniquely melodic role, with short riffs above the chords of the rhythm guitar, without distracting from everything else like a lead guitar might—or, with bands like Primus, bass could take the lead. I figured I could handle Wes' inevitable jokes about the stoner bassist stereotype.

When eighth grade began, there were a couple of immediate differences from the last. First was that our band teacher had moved after the end of the last school year, and the new teacher had never taught middle school students before. He had the incorrect expectation that we would be focused and act serious all of the time. Unprepared to handle the reality of a bunch of thirteen-year-olds saying and doing stupid shit at inconvenient moments, he got so angry on multiple occasions that he just gave up, and shut himself in his office for the remainder of the class. This was in no small part due to Wes, and by extension, myself, and unfortunately our teacher would have to see us as many as three times every day.

Wes and I continued to play saxophone in the symphonic and jazz bands, while also signing up to play a new instrument in concert band. We did this mostly to avoid the other terrible "elective" classes available, which were not actually elective in any sense of choice—the term only meant that the classes didn't give any required credits. Wes wanted to play trumpet, so I shrugged and went along with it. I probably would have tried bass clarinet, otherwise.

The jazz band also had a bass guitar position, which had been vacated with last year's player entering high school. I wanted to audition, but even if I had been good enough to get the spot, that didn't guarantee that I wouldn't screw up when actually performing the parts. It wasn't such a big deal to pick up trumpet, because the concert band songs were pretty simple, and like ten other people were playing the same part, at the same time, on the same instrument. The people in jazz band tended to be pretty good at their instruments, and I wasn't sure if I was good enough at playing bass yet. What really sealed the deal was that I had learned to play bass with guitar tabs, but for jazz band I would have to read sheet music in bass clef, which I hadn't done with any instrument yet. Since the audition included sight reading—playing a song at full-speed while looking at the sheet music for the first time—I used that as a great excuse not to audition. Why bother to risk the embarrassment, when I was already going to be playing saxophone for a third year, anyway?

The other thing that was very different about eighth grade was how focused our teachers were on high school. It felt like they almost neglected teaching their own subjects, to lecture us on how different high school was going to be, and to declare that we would suffer if we did not "prepare" in very non-specific ways. The classes were going to be unimaginably more difficult, and require infinitely more out-of-class work; the teachers would have zero tolerance for anyone who was not completely focused all of the time; and the older teens would view freshmen as being of a lesser species than themselves. Teachers also liked to point out, like my parents always had, that your grades and behavior in high school would define the remainder of your pitiful life. As you can imagine, in spite of knowing through my sister that these were exaggerations, these frequent rants did wonders for my anxiety, making me wonder if I really was hopelessly stupid and childish.

An honors science class that was offered also had some fancy label I can't remember, which meant that it would give students who passed it a high school science credit. It was clearer to me than ever that, regardless of what I thought about myself, everyone else was going to think I was lazy and shortsighted, if nothing else, for not taking an opportunity like that, so I signed up for it.

It was a bizarre experience; one minute, the teacher was highly inclined to rant about how hellish high school was going to be if we weren't ready, and the next, she was playing a *Looney Tunes* clip, supposedly in order to demonstrate a physics concept.

Not far into the year, my body decided it was time to hurry up and finish puberty. My voice closed in on its deep monotone while still cracking all the time, my upper lip and chin sprouted a handful of hairs, my awkward gait became more exaggerated as I tried to account for a sudden increase in height, and I was still becoming attracted to girls whom I had previously not been, making my existing anxieties that much more encompassing.

One of these girls was in band, and a friend of Wes'; as such, I quickly developed the ability to discreetly ditch Wes, and look busy elsewhere, whenever she headed in our direction. My success in avoiding ever speaking to her, however, was not to last. One day, Wes and I were hanging around outside alone, probably after school while waiting for some band event, when this girl and another of her friends came around a corner and greeted us. Even my panicking brain knew that I wasn't going to worm my way out of this conversation, so I instead opted for the deer-in-headlights approach, my face frozen in whatever expression it had been in when I had first noticed them.

The plan, more or less, was to nod along to whatever anybody was saying, and chuckle if Wes laughed at something. These girls were Wes' friends, so they'd have no reason to say anything specifically to me, right? Well, that's not how most people's brains work, and of course the girl I liked asked me a direct question. Unfortunately, I can't tell you what it was, because I now have no idea. I did comprehend it at the time, and attempted to offer some sort of reply, but as my brain was already vacating the premises, I stuttered something verging on nonsense. I have very little recollection of the rest of the encounter, but I think everyone else awkwardly giggled, and someone changed the subject, before Wes thankfully came up with an out for us. He never said anything about it, and I never talked about it with anyone. I was extremely embarrassed, and promised myself that I would never again end up in a situation I couldn't get out of. I think this was the only time I ever spoke something resembling words to someone I was attracted to.

Obviously, I now realize that many people go through this sort of experience, and what I needed to do was keep trying. But, though that social situation was anything but unique, my own experiences and thought processes certainly were, as are everyone's, and they guided my behavior. My thought process always started with someone else: would that girl really want to talk to me? She might have thought she did—or she might have just been being polite.

Besides, I knew I didn't really have anything to offer. I was nice enough, smart enough, but in friendships, I tended to just be a vessel for other people to bounce thoughts or jokes off of, and anybody can do that. Unless someone insisted on getting to know me, like all my friends had, I didn't see the point in bothering them. I didn't think it was fair to do it just because I wanted to, and while I did have self-esteem at this point, it was never enough that I saw myself as being impressive or interesting.

And, the truth was, it wasn't just my anxiety that caused me not to want to talk to her; it was the root of my anxiety—the lack of social skills. I hadn't been taught things like how to express my emotions, and I hadn't been comfortable (or perhaps uncomfortable) enough to try figuring that out on my own in sixth grade, so why should things be any different, two years later? I could kind of hold conversations with people that insisted on it, but had no chance of starting or carrying them on my own.

Even if none of that had mattered to me, I didn't really understand what I could gain by talking to a girl I liked. Maybe I'd end up being friends with her, like Wes was, but I was already comfortable with the friends I had, and as a thirteen-year-old boy, the prospect of being friends with someone I was attracted to sounded horrifyingly awkward. Maybe if I kept trying with a person I liked, I'd find someone that really liked me, and we could have a different kind of relationship.

But I thought I knew how that sort of relationship would turn out. Right now, it would turn out like my sister's short, awkward relationships with boys she thought she liked, which ended up leaving her sad or frustrated. Maybe that was just because she was still a kid, barely any older than me. Maybe it was worth trying, just to figure out what didn't work. Maybe then, as an adult, I could figure out how, and why, to make a relationship like that work.

But I'd seen how that ended up with my own parents, too, and I'd read enough divorce statistics to know that about half of the couples that decided they loved each other—enough to promise it forever—had been a little off, to say the least. I began to believe that, while I could certainly feel attracted to girls, and while I could appreciate anyone for their personality, I would never be able to feel love. It was an emotion that I began to unconsciously associate with deliberate self-delusion, hypocritical selfishness, and the sickening sensation of a trust I felt my parents had broken—with myself, my siblings, and with each other.

My association of P.E. classes with being harassed by jocks was more conscious than ever. In eighth grade, we'd sometimes play handball, which, as someone who has less than zero interest in it, I would explain as being soccer with your hands, or dodgeball where whichever poor bastard is closest to the goal-net isn't supposed to dodge anymore. If, like myself at the time, you haven't heard of it, you might think that random middle schoolers playing it sounds like a great way to end up with a kid's fingers broken. Or maybe that's just me, since one of the school's basketball players flung a ball at me at top speed while I was assigned as goalie, which resulted in me breaking the fifth finger of my left hand in attempting to block it.

Well, I did succeed in blocking the goal, so I didn't get laughed at for that, at least. I did get laughed at for crying in pain, so still probably not worth it. I didn't have to participate in P.E. for a while, which was some consolation, but I also couldn't play bass or saxophone with all my fingers. A doctor had good news for me, at least: by putting a metal pin in the finger via surgery, he could point it somewhat back in the right direction, and I might even be able to flex it. It would cost about $14,000, but after insurance, it would only be a couple thousand or so! Welcome to America. I got to take a day off school to get my finger cut open, and I'm well aware of how fortunate I was that my dad was able to afford it.

After wearing a brace for a while, I finally got to see how well my finger was going to work after all that. On the bright side, I could move it. Unfortunately, it could barely apply enough pressure to push a saxophone key or depress a bass string, felt weird when doing so, and the fingertip pointed almost towards the center of my palm. The doctor shrugged and recommended me a physical therapist, whom I ended up seeing only once out of frustration and anxiety. I kept doing the exercises she recommended at home for a year or so, and saw some improvement, but it remains somewhat bent and impotent even now. The experience made me feel that trying to fit in, doing the things that normal kids did, would only make it more outwardly obvious that I didn't, and only make things more painful for myself, on multiple levels.

In any case, I was able to continue playing saxophone at the same level before too much longer, if a bit cautiously. I was the first chair saxophone in symphonic band at that point, which also meant that I was first chair in jazz band. I was informed by the teacher not long before a concert that this meant I would be expected to stand up on cue during one of the jazz tunes, and improvise a solo of indeterminate duration, over only a handful of backing instruments. I optimistically asked the teacher if I could maybe just write a solo ahead of time. He laughed, and told me that improvising was half of the fun of playing jazz. Maybe, I thought, that was why I did not like jazz.

Wes responded in his usual dramatically-enthusiastic manner, halfway teasing me about it, and halfway trying to hype me up for it. I was a little excited, and very much terrified. I practiced every night, making sure I had memorized the key and tempo of the song perfectly, so I could play something that was varied, melodically and rhythmically, while still following the song.

I doubt that I had ever been more anxious than I was on the day of that concert. I spent most of the school day trying not to vomit, just nodding or forcing a smile each time Wes saw fit to insert some remark about the concert. The time arrived, and as concert band always played first, I walked onto stage with a trumpet for the first time. I screwed up a few times, but the ten or so other trumpet players meant that it was completely unnoticeable. At the conclusion of the last song, Wes and I half-sprinted off the stage to put up our trumpets, sort through a pile of sheet music, and put together our saxophones. That takes longer than you'd think, especially when you're anxious and can't find a reed that isn't broken, nor line it up on the mouthpiece.

Lips still tingling from the trumpet mouthpiece, I played a few quiet notes just offstage to make sure I still knew how a saxophone worked, before we had to head back out for symphonic band. Those songs were the most technically difficult we had to play that night by far, but it wasn't anything written on sheet music that I was figuratively pissing my pants about at that moment. After we were done, I thought about how much I missed sitting in the audience, screwing around for part of the concert. I even missed the frantic instrument-swap from a little while ago. I impatiently waited offstage, while Wes continued to run his mouth in the usual manner.

Finally, we were directed to go onstage, and we began. Each slow, swung-rhythm jazz song felt slower and swing-ier than the last. Then, that song began. I played most of it very quietly, saving my lips and lungs for the moment of truth. In spite of knowing exactly when my solo was supposed to be, I stared daggers at the teacher, waiting for him to direct me to rise. As he gestured at me, I shot up like my ass was on fire, almost shoving my chair into the person behind me and knocking my music stand over simultaneously. Wes lunged, preventing both disasters without a snicker.

I then played a solo that felt way too long, before I was finally directed to return to my seat, and received a round of applause as we finished the song. It was finally over. Wes resumed his role as hypeman as we put our instruments away. It was hard not to smile at least a little bit, but I really didn't want to think about it anymore. I grabbed an instrument case with each hand, jamming the piles of sheet music between the handles, and sped-walk into the audience in search of whichever parent was giving me a ride home, trying with limited success to change the subject of my family's conversation, upon being met with my mom's inevitable saxophone-induced excitement.

I felt like I needed to let my thoughts about it stew for a few days. Even then, my feelings remained mixed. I felt like I had done a nice job; my mom had unsurprisingly enjoyed it, and Wes certainly enjoyed ranting about how good it was, in his usual inscrutable level-of-seriousness. But I had not done it without feeling really uncomfortable, and really, what did it accomplish? Then again, it didn't have to accomplish anything, any more than all of the other concerts had. It was supposed to be fun. I guess I never figured out whether it actually was fun, or not. In some ways, it feels like it was the last time, for a very long time, that I really had mixed feelings about anything.

While I was finishing this chapter, I asked James about a particular joke I remembered Wes having made, as I couldn't recall when it had happened. He told me that it was during an eighth grade honor band trip, where the three of us, among others from our school, were performing at a district level. It entailed an overnight stay somewhere, and I roomed with the two of them. Even after being reminded, I barely remember that this ever happened. I performed at quite a few events, throughout seventh and eighth grade, which I can't even describe, because I remember so little about them. I think I have some ribbons and trophies in a box, buried in a closet somewhere. It's a bit sad to realize that I can barely recall what were probably the biggest events of my life just over a decade ago, thanks to the cloud of my anxiety.

DISSONANCE TO MY EARS

The end of eighth grade was generally foreboding. It was almost time to start at a new school, the youngest once again. The terror that high school supposedly would be had been instilled into me—not specifically in the way that the ranting teachers alluded to, but in the way that I felt that new things always were, hammered home with each passing class. Home life had been getting steadily more stressful; summer break wasn't the same as before, but I was still looking forward to it.

But there was a surprise in store for the summer. Near the end of the year, the band teacher informed us that the eighth graders were invited to visit the high school, to hang out and play some stand tunes with the marching band. That sounded horrible to me, but as you might have been able to guess, Wes thought it sounded like the best thing ever, and begged me to come. Lacking in willpower as usual, I gave in.

The event did anything but make me want to join marching band. Watching football for hours from the stands, and occasionally playing obnoxious school spirit songs, sounded plenty bad enough. That, of course, was the least of it, compared to the halftime shows. Just the thought of playing saxophone for a stadium full of disinterested high school students, while simultaneously marching in formation—especially as someone who had to focus to walk in a straight line— made me so anxious I thought I might have a stroke. Even that wasn't all—there were trips, competitions, and a parade through downtown that we had to play in.

But, if you haven't figured it out yet, Wes pleaded with me to join anyway, and I did. I was so certain that I did not want to, that if he had been the only one telling me to do it, I might have actually managed to resist. Unfortunately, my sister had joined color guard two years earlier, and had spent most of the time since gushing about how amazing marching band was. Between her, my parents, and Wes, I never heard the end of it, and once again, I did what everyone else told me I should, as if I was incapable of determining what I wanted on my own. This regrettable decision of mine, if you can call it that, had one more catch to it. I had to spend two weeks of my summer at "band camp", which meant going to the high school football field every day, in the nearly-one-hundred-degree weather, to learn marching technique. Well, if high school was really going to be so horrible, at least I would be getting a head-start.

With the last day at the middle school came an obligatory outdoor party-thing for the eighth grade. At one point, I ended up standing around alone. I don't remember why; maybe others had left early, which hadn't been an option for me, or maybe different classes had gone outside at different times. Then, the most confusing thing that had so far occurred in my life took place in under a minute. A girl I had known (or more accurately, known of) since elementary school approached me and greeted me by name, which already had me with my eyebrows raised in confusion. I responded, and asked her what was up. She quickly divulged that her friend "liked" me—pointing this friend out, who was standing alone nearby, looking the other way—and that this friend wanted to ask me something to the effect of whether I'd like to go out with her.

I suspect that the look of utter incomprehension in my eyes said it all, but I also turned bright red, and before my brain could think of something better, I blurted out "No, thanks," in a tone that probably sounded like disgust. I immediately felt bad, but my brain was still processing what had just happened, and I just walked off, and picked a less conspicuous spot for standing around alone. In fairness to myself, asking someone out for someone else is a very awkward-middle-schooler thing to do, and most people would not know how to respond to that. On top of that, I hadn't even known the girl's name until about five seconds earlier, and had only so much as seen her from a distance a handful of times. Nonetheless, I was extremely embarrassed about how rude my response had been—and I realized how much more embarrassing it must have been to be on the other end of that. Any consideration I had left towards ever trying to talk to someone I liked was rapidly evaporating.

Every day of the summer break felt like it lasted a week, as anxieties of the coming year occupied me more constantly than ever. And yet, it seemed that no more than a week could have passed when the part of summer I had to myself was gone, and marching band practice began. I focused mostly on not passing out in the heat, and was at least successful by that metric. The music we'd be playing was pretty simple, which made sense given that we had to memorize it, along with the nerd equivalent of a dance routine for every song.

Feeling stressed, sick, and bored out of my mind was an exhausting combination, and one that would only be significantly worse once I had to spend my Friday nights doing it in front of a jury of my peers. Of course, such an embarrassment would never be complete without a hideous and overheating uniform to fit the mood. In a disquieting turn of events, I was almost looking forward to high school now, because I was pretty sure there was no way it could be worse than twenty-four/seven marching band. The only other thing left before school was my physical exam—required by my state in order to participate in marching band—which would end up being the last time I visited a general doctor as of the time I'm writing this.

In a feeling reminiscent of sixth grade, my first day of high school began with a cartographic sort of panic. In spite of already having visited all of my classrooms during the "open house" event a few days ago, I was terrified that I was going to forget how to find them. I stared at my schedule, crumpled from having been stuffed into a pocket, and tried to remember which direction to go for every hall or disconnected room. It didn't help—I was too distracted. There were people everywhere, already talking and laughing in pairs or groups. It was sensorially overwhelming, and I did all I could not to stand out, leaning against a wall alone. I kept glancing around anxiously for any sign of someone I knew, whom I did not end up finding until classes began.

Through the first few days, though, it became clear that most of the supposed terrors of high school had been exaggerated. Though many seniors were indeed imposing, particularly boys that now had the heights and hairs of men, they did not seem concerned with flaunting their superiority over freshmen, as my middle school teachers had warned us they would. And, while classes were certainly more difficult, that had more to do with the quantity of work, rather than with some inscrutability inherent to high school curriculum.

Our schedules now divided into four class periods rather than six, teachers crammed as much content as they could into the resultantly longer classes. I had never had a particularly impressive attention span, and the main thing that had kept me focused in middle school—or at least awake—was having to get up, walk around, and do something different every hour or so. It had been plenty challenging anyway, since my sleep loss from anxiety had progressively worsened. Around the start of ninth grade, I also started having vertigo while in the dark, and eventually had to start keeping the lights on at night, making it that much harder to go to sleep. Coming to school tired every day, and then having to sit in one chair for ninety minutes at a time, made it hard to resist the urge to take naps.

I tried very hard to stay awake, fearing that if I fell asleep, I would end up being awoken and embarrassed by an angry teacher. One day, extremely tired and in my second-to-last class, I finally drifted off, and woke in a panic five minutes before the bell. As soon as class ended, I caught up to whom we'll call Samuel—a new student to the area who had made my acquaintance—and embarrassedly told him that I had fallen asleep, and begged him to summarize what I had missed. Samuel, both extremely intelligent and ceaselessly focused, half-jokingly shamed me for falling asleep in class, then offered an abstract summary of the high-level concepts that he thought the teacher had been trying to explain, which, though completely useless, was at least concise.

I was briefly terrified that I was doomed to fail our next handful of assignments in the class and embarrass myself. It was only when I got home and looked at our homework assignment that I realized—I didn't need a teacher, or a textbook, because I had the internet. In fact, reverse-engineering my homework to figure out what I was supposed to have learned in class was actually a lot easier than listening to a teacher ramble for an hour and a half.

Still, the real fear I had of falling asleep had little to do with classwork, and more to do with being embarrassed in front of the class if a teacher noticed. I continued fighting to remain awake, especially in my Advanced Placement (AP) classes. These classes would conclude with an exam, written by the College Board, administered in a location separate from the school. Kids that scored highly enough on the exam (which, uniquely, was always scored relative to how others had done that year) would receive a credit for a college course, allowing them to get a degree and start a career faster. As far as I knew, this was the end goal of life, and so I expected that these classes would be both very important and very difficult. Really, they were just like any other class, but they went through material faster, and included more large, project-type assignments. Even as I realized that, my anxiety over potential failure continued to increase. My sister, now a junior in high school, already had plenty of college credits under her belt. I knew my parents expected me to do just as well; they had made it clear how my life would turn out if I did—and if I did not.

Expectations were really the difference between middle school and high school. No, the atmosphere of my classes was not one of somber focus, as my eighth grade teachers had insisted it would be; there was still plenty of goofing off by kids, teachers going on tangents totally unrelated to class, and everything in-between. But some of the teachers were not shy in talking about how they viewed success. When the class laughed at someone who was joking around, the teacher would laugh, too, but they'd make sure to follow up with some pointed remark about who's going to get into college, and who's going to work at a fast food drive-thru. That would make even the biggest class clown blush before offering a retort.

Seeing someone else get comments like that was stressful enough for me. It just reinforced the worry that was already there that I wouldn't be able to push through and succeed. Being called out in that way, myself, would be extremely embarrassing. The teachers' words were intended to be a form of negative reinforcement: if kids fear the consequences of not trying, then they'll try harder. But what I saw was the immediate consequence of standing out—a reminder that your worth is defined by your success, and a shaming for any happiness that might distract from that. Sure, that made me care more about not failing— but it also didn't give me anything to look forward to; a reason to succeed.

I began to feel conflicted—I've always known I'm supposed to work hard in school to have a better, easier life, but why does everyone seem to connect that life with a complete lack of chill, or any kind of joy? The tentative comfort I had begun to develop with expressing myself in seventh and eighth grade began to recede. I became a much quieter person—much like I had been before I started to really appreciate friendships during middle school, but now, I was conscious of my reservation. When my friends wanted to talk or mess around in class, I tended to respond quickly and quietly, or just hush them instead. It wasn't because I was consumed with my success in class, nor that I didn't want to talk to my friends anymore—it was because I didn't want to face the shame of being the guy that went through life the wrong way.

The one class I really did care about, far more than any AP, was Web Design. Even though I didn't have any interest in web design specifically, it was my first opportunity to take a technology-related class that wasn't about learning how to use a keyboard. I was finally graded on something that was at least tangentially related to the career I imagined for myself, which, at the time, was video game programming. The class was a window of time for me to calm down amidst my daily anxieties. I had learned HTML and design basics on my own time already, so I felt confident in completing assignments, without having to worry about focusing on a lesson.

The teacher was one of the best I ever had. He would joke around, and not take anything too seriously, while still making sure everyone understood what he was teaching. He talked to kids like they were friends, as much as students—I remember talking to him once about the music I liked, which wasn't something I was comfortable talking about with anyone other than James and Chris, who liked similar stuff. He also complimented my classwork with genuine enthusiasm, while also pointing out things I had room to improve on, in a way that felt like he wasn't telling me to fix mistakes, but rather to improve what was already good. Rather than feeling like I was just getting the same decent understanding of a subject as everyone else in the class, I felt like I might actually be able to make something uniquely awesome. Eventually, he started asking me to help other students with coding questions, and I was more comfortable doing that than I had ever imagined I could be—still anxious over my ability to explain something well, but confident that, at least, I knew what I was trying to say.

At the opposite pole, in some ways, was German class. My school required that every student take at least two foreign language classes (usually, two levels of the same language) before they could graduate. My sister had chosen German in her sophomore year, and now was obsessed with it, choosing to continue onto the higher level classes. Since most people tended to get at least the first required level done in ninth grade, I decided to get it over with, rather than make it more awkward later. I had no language preference of my own, so when my sister enthused about how awesome German was, I went with it, after making sure at least a couple of my friends were good with doing the same.

On the positive side, I was in the class with James and Wes, and got to work mostly with them whenever we had to do something in a group. The teacher was nice, too, if a little blunt. But, given that we were learning a language, we would eventually have to speak it. Sure, I could manage practicing the pronunciation of specific words, mumbling along with the rest of the class, or just mouthing silently if I was really anxious that day. Naturally, though, we would inevitably have to prove to the teacher—and often, the whole class—that we had, in fact, learned how to speak in complete sentences.

The anxieties I had over class participation in other subjects were both constant and magnified in German —I could barely mumble out complete sentences when asked to answer questions in my native language. We were all terrible at German-accented pronunciation—I was far from the worst, and most everyone laughed at everyone else's attempts—but, already being extremely self-conscious of the way words fell out of my mouth when not prepared well in advance, I felt humiliated every time I had to speak.

A feeling developed throughout the first half of ninth grade that I was actually getting more awkward at expressing myself. The language I was speaking didn't matter; it was the sound of my voice, my mannerisms, and maybe even some parts of my core personality. That's how it felt, as classmates around me seemed to lose all their inhibitions. Even the most stereotypical of the jocks—the sort that seemed like they failed English classes just for fun, and were already bragging about spending their weekends hammered—had an easier time getting people to understand them than I did. I just didn't know why.

I realized that I definitely didn't have any problem understanding other people: their emotional expressions, and their expectations of others, but even their subtle, perhaps unconscious, mannerisms, that seemed to tell me what they were thinking, even before it might have occurred to them to say it. Constant anxiety at school and home had taught me to look for the signs that immediately said so much about how others were feeling, and I found them everywhere now, with a persistent, unconscious effort. It seemed like everyone should be so approachable, like I knew just what I could say, and how I should say it; yet, when the time came for me to open my mouth, all the eyes on me felt so much colder.

Samuel would be the first and last relatively close friend I made during high school. It was so much effort to even feign a basic level of comfort with someone new who had chosen to speak to me that, unconsciously, I stopped trying to. Anxiety, and exasperation at myself, began to slip into the tone of even my one-word responses. This is no better illustrated than in my memories of marching band, which had continued without pause with the school year's beginning. The daily class mostly entailed practicing the music inside, and occasionally practicing some marching techniques in the bus loop, right outside. It eventually became mostly a period of free time, which was more than welcome, since we also had multiple after-school practices per week.

The rigor intensified over the hours on the field, as the first football game of the season approached. The band director, discerning which major mistakes were not going to fix themselves, descended upon a poor soul or two in particular for ten or fifteen minutes at a time, leaving the rest of the band plenty of time to stand around in their places and chat. I knew about half of the saxophone players, being friends with Wes, and having met those from the grade above me while in the symphonic and jazz bands in seventh grade; the other half were juniors and seniors. I didn't dislike any of them, but neither did I particularly relish the opportunities like these to hang out with them.

These small interactions on the field, though, consisted mostly of people complaining about how late they'd have to be up finishing homework that night, if the trombone players didn't hurry up and learn how to march. The class period was worse, in that sense: once the ever-shortening rehearsal at the beginning of class had concluded, most people just hung out and screwed around. Anything but interested in that, I looked for a corner to compress myself in, hoping that everyone would get the hint. That didn't always happen, with Wes or a sophomore sax player growing bored and heading over for some small talk. I tried to ignore my anxiety over these potential interactions enough to work on my homework, often including that which was due within the next two hours—neglected in my lacking abilities to concentrate, or even rest.

Soon, football season began, and the halftime show was as good as it was going to get. In the practices leading up to our first performance, we reviewed what we'd be doing for the remainder of every three-hour football game. This included two parts: watching football and/or referee deliberations for a while, and then dramatically performing one of a handful of brief school spirit tunes, on cue in response to whatever was happening.

I guess I had assumed that most of the band was here for the halftime show performance, and just put up with the rest. I was now beginning to realize that I was misguided. About half of the sax section seemed to genuinely enjoy the prospect of cheering on the football team. The rest still had plenty of fun blaring out the immensely-grating stand tunes, and swinging their instruments as if attempting to uppercut the skull of the person in front of them. I felt completely out-of-place already, playing as loudly as possible without reservation, trying to dance as if I didn't care how stupidly overzealous I would look to the people in the stands that could see us.

Evidently, I stood out every bit as much as I felt like I would. It only took a couple of fifteen-second songs into our first rehearsal in the stands for someone to point it out. A senior sax player—a nice guy, but my polar opposite as far as energy and extroversion went—was the first. Smiling wider than I had believed a human capable, he half-yelled something encouraging me to "get into it", and slapped me on the back. All the other sax players looked over. Wes and one of the sophomores that knew me laughed, probably realizing that I was not about to get into it. We went through another song almost immediately, and if anything, I was less into it. Doing things I liked alright and was decent at, like playing my instrument, was uncomfortable enough with eyes on me. "Horn flashing", as marching bands call dancing with an instrument, was not one of these things, and was far worse.

As we finished up the rehearsal, the section leader approached me, and informed me earnestly that I should "have more fun" with it, as that was the point. I mumbled something about how it wasn't really my thing and walked off. Wes and the sophomore thought my unenthusiasm, having attracted that much attention, was hilarious. I wasn't at all comfortable talking about my anxiety, so I just played into their idea that I was participating minimally because I hated football so much. I truly did, so it wasn't hard to pretend that was the real reason, and keep my anxiety to myself.

I had never looked forward to something less than I did that first football game, and I had a near-constant stomach ache in the days leading up to it. The day arrived; having barely slept that night and feeling like trash, I dozed lightly through about half of my classes, and spent the others trying to massage the headache out of my forehead. I ate nothing the entire day before the game, other than part of a small snack at lunch, just so people wouldn't ask me why I wasn't eating.

After the school day, the afternoon, and the trip back to the school, which each felt eternal, there were only a few precious minutes of milling around anxiously before it was time to file into the football stands. Shortly, the football team headed onto the field, and we were directed to play one of the stand tunes at the top of our lungs. My breathing already shallow, I pressed my keys along to the song without pushing any air through the instrument. This went entirely unnoticed, everyone else more than loud enough to make up for me.

My horn flashing, however, more lackluster than usual due to my suspicion that I would puke on someone if I moved too much, was called out once again, as the ecstatic people around me reminded me, specifically by name, to "get into it!" and "have fun!" I turned red with a combination of embarrassment and exasperation, not so much as turning to face the encouragement, pretending I hadn't heard over all the people cheering nearby.

The game proceeded at a snail's pace, which was an unwelcome surprise for someone that hadn't watched enough football before to realize just how much downtime it necessitated. Finally, the team left the field for halftime, and soon, the band director was beckoning us down like the Grim Reaper. Trying to stop my limbs from shaking, I followed my section down towards the field, swallowing the stomach acid entering my mouth.

I don't remember much about that halftime show, or really any of them. I remember how hot it was then, and how cold it was in December. I remember having to stare up at the crowds as I marched, crossing my eyes a little so I couldn't discern individual faces. I remember occasionally going one step too far in a particular direction, before panicking to get back into my spot. I remember when it was finally over, and thankfully, how little attention everyone in the stands seemed to be paying to us as we exited the field.

Then, it was time for another ninety minutes or so of mostly nothing, interspersed with stand tunes. At least some of my anxiety was overridden by exhaustion and irritation. When it finally ended, we walked back to the band room, most people in high spirits, some yelling about whatever the outcome of the football game had been. I stuffed my sax back into the case and leaned against a wall vaguely near wherever Wes had wanted to go, rubbing my eyes as I waited for my sister to finish effusing to her color guard friends about how awesome their performance had been, so she could drive us home.

That was how most of my weekends would start for the rest of that semester. Eventually, at least, people quit telling me to be more enthusiastic in the stands. I would like to think they realized they were only making me more anxious, but since I was never able to tell them anything to that effect, they probably just thought I was being stubborn and rude. I felt so stupid for having agreed to join. It didn't matter that other people had wanted me to do it; it didn't even matter that I had never wanted to. I simply couldn't do it. I couldn't keep feeling so sick all the time. I couldn't keep reliving the shame I felt—for not being able to do what everyone else insisted was fun and easy.

Unfortunately, I also couldn't quit. Even if it hadn't been unrealistic to ask to switch classes that late into the semester, I couldn't have faced all the questions about why I'd given up on something I'd chosen to do. I pushed on, making it through each game one at a time, desperately clinging to the hope that it would get easier, but only feeling that it was getting harder. It seemed that simply exposing myself to the things that caused me the most anxiety was not enough to normalize them to me.

I couldn't express my anxiety to my parents in any meaningful way. They just didn't get it. They would assume it was just tied to specific events, like halftime shows, and that I'd get used to them. When I tried to explain the persistent, sickening feelings of dread and shame that I suffered, and from so many small, different things, they told me it was normal, and I'd grow out of it. I tried so hard to make them understand, or at least accept, the differences that were beginning to emerge in how I acted towards them, with my intensifying anxiety.

I needed more personal space and time, more mental privacy, and as little public interaction as possible; I needed them to accept my low emotional state, and to be patient with my scattered thoughts. I needed them to trust that my difficulties in interacting with them weren't because I was ignoring them, or because I hated them, but because, for so many reasons, interacting with anyone had become something that required so much effort. But they didn't understand my issues, and they didn't accept the things that I needed. Dad was always irked when I had to be reminded of something I'd forgotten to do, or when it made me so anxious to go in a store with him. Mom never stopped getting offended when I didn't feel up to pretending to be happy or excited, or to talk about my terrible day, or to give her a hug. No words I could say ever made a difference.

During my time in marching band, I was far more anxious and unhappy than I had ever been, but there was some sort of a bright side. There was a sophomore french horn player, whom we'll call Will, whom I had been around occasionally since seventh grade, due to his friendship with one of the sax players, who was also in the year ahead of me. At some point during marching band, Will caught wind of the fact that I played bass guitar, and that I liked the idea of playing in a metal

band, but didn't know of two interested guitarists—
Chris played a bit and was down, but Isaac wasn't into
the idea. I don't remember how Will heard, exactly, but
he must have either overheard me talking to Chris, or
heard it from his sophomore sax friend.

Either way, it turned out that Will also liked metal,
and played guitar. He asked if I knew anyone else that
would want to be in a band, and I told him about Chris,
as well as James, who had started playing drum kit for
jazz band a couple years earlier. So, in a move that felt
both uncharacteristic and completely predictable, when
Will, whom I barely knew, offered to play lead guitar, I
took him up on it. To some extent, I guess I thought my
anxiety couldn't really get any worse at the time, so I
might as well use the opportunity to try something new
that I was actually interested in.

But truthfully, that was more of a post-justification
—I didn't think it through, at all, at the time. I
panicked, and answered automatically. I still had
enough self-esteem then that, when it mixed with my
anxiety over others' expectations of me, I guess I
believed that the best way to keep people from disliking
me was to never say no. My fear of being criticized was
already very high, but I had enough confidence in my
own strengths to believe that the best way to avoid the
shame of judgment was to prove I was above it. Even if
I wasn't sure I was, saying no would have meant failing
to reach expectations without even having tried.

So, with the band director's permission, our new
group started practicing in the band room some days
after school. We learned a few cover songs, and
eventually added a couple that I'd written. It was
something fun to look forward to for a while, but it did

not come without bringing its share of anxiety. Since it had been my idea, I was put in charge of scheduling our practices, deciding what we were playing, making sure everyone understood their parts, and whatever else. As you might have caught on to, I am not a very assertive person, even when I am in a comfortable situation. My plan, therefore, was to hope that everyone was on the same page, and that if they weren't, that they'd bring that up.

Well, that didn't happen. I was hoping to start a relatively serious band, which wrote and played some cool songs, and figure out if that was something I would enjoy or not. James generally went along with that, but I don't think he cared about the music, as much as he did about helping me do something I wanted. Chris had only started playing guitar recently, and didn't have a whole lot of time or space to practice; I think he mostly wanted to hang out with us and jam. I didn't know Will well at all, but I had gotten the impression, from the way he acted in band classes throughout the years, that he would want to take the music seriously. In practice, while he was probably the most talented of us on his instrument, he didn't seem very interested in providing any input on what we were doing; nor did he always learn the parts I wrote, even after insisting he was going to, even after passing on my offers to cut or simplify things like guitar solos. He already had a lot going on, and I think he realized he had taken on a bit more than he really wanted to, but didn't want to admit that.

Resultantly, our practices were a mess. Once everyone had shown up, I would make an awkward attempt at leadership, asking everyone specifically whether they had worked on the parts they were supposed to be learning, to which I usually received a combination of unconfident "yes" answers and frank "no"'s. Regardless, there was usually nothing to do but give the songs a shot. At first, I would attempt to politely and embarrassedly point out mistakes anyone had made after a song was done, starting with my own. Usually, this would lead to vacant nods in response, before one of the two I wasn't specifically talking to would get distracted and start talking with the other about marching band, or a teacher that had annoyed them, or *Skyrim*, or any random joke or gossip that came to mind.

Since we never made any real progress, it was kind of pointless to play through any song more than once or twice, and it was clearly futile to try adding another one. Each time, it would soon become clear that everyone was more interested in chatting or screwing around than continuing to proverbially smash our heads into the wall, and I'd just give up and join them. I'm not saying I didn't have fun switching instruments around until I ended up playing the drum part for "Smells Like Teen Spirit" or "Down with the Sickness", but it wasn't exactly what I had signed up for. I'm sure the band director felt the same way when he walked in one such day, and I had to attempt to come up with a good explanation for why the bassist was bludgeoning the school's cymbals.

Before these experiences, I had felt that my social shortcomings would eventually stop mattering. Social situations would probably always cause me anxiety, and my inability to express my emotions would probably limit my relationships to friends that hung out exclusively because of shared interests or sense of humor, but did any of that really matter? After I graduated college, I could just start a career as a game programmer, hang out with other socially awkward dudes with the same hobbies, and call it a life.

But as my interests led me to start my first band, I began to see the problem with this idea: communication is key in virtually everything. Everyone that participates in something with someone else has to be able to calmly and earnestly express themselves— their perspective, goals, preferences, and feelings—to everyone else. Otherwise, someone will end up uncomfortable, unhappy, or disappointed, at the very least, and these feelings tend to be infectious. I don't think any of us really got what we wanted out of playing together. We had fun sometimes, but it never really stopped being awkward and frustrating. If I couldn't communicate well enough to have fun just sharing an interest with my friends, maybe I'd be better off sticking to things I could do alone.

But at least until the end of the semester, I was stuck doing things with a whole bunch of other people. After most, if not all, of the football games came the marching band competition. With no game, and no expectation of stand tunes, the actual competition would be at least a little less painful. Maybe more members of the audience would actually be watching, belonging to marching bands of other schools, but they also didn't know me, and would never see me again, and it did help me to know that at the time.

Regardless, everything surrounding the event did more than enough to make up for any anxiety deficit I might have had. For one thing, getting a high score at competition seemed to be the band director's sole desire in life, and he was not shy about imposing the importance he attached to it on the kids responsible for earning it for him. I had generally been doing alright, and wasn't personally concerned that I would bring him shame, but I had been around high-strung people enough for his furrowed brows and momentary glares at others to make me plenty anxious.

The location of the competition was far more discomforting. To reach it would require a bus ride of multiple hours, directly before and after the hours-long event. At least we would get to have some input on our bus seats, but that was little solace. I knew from experience I didn't really want to hang out with anyone for that long, even my friends of four years or more, and that was before everyone else came into the equation, especially during the drive over.

Unfortunately, I had already made my choice when I signed up for marching band, so on the bus I went. Chris ended up on a different bus; I was with Wes. My usual stomach aching had begun hours ago, and I could only hope that I wouldn't actually get sick for the duration of the ride, as hours of anxiety mixed with hours of motion sickness. Napping through the trip, or at least pretending to, would have been preferable, but I had too much of a headache to close my eyes. I alternated between leaning my head against the window and the back of the seat in front of me, trying my best to make it clear that I was a poor candidate for conversation. It worked somewhat, but most of the people around me were constantly twisting in different directions, looking for anyone else who would listen to them point out weird people in cars nearby, or tell a joke, or say whatever else that came to mind to entertain themselves.

We finally arrived, the contents of my stomach still churning, but still in place. Filing off the buses, we joined a long line waiting to enter the event area, as the bands were all checked in. Our section leader approached Wes and I, the only freshmen sax players, to ask if we were excited for our first competition. I would have usually just let Wes answer, then nodded along, but for once, he just answered with brief and unenthusiastic words of agreement. He preferred goofing off in the stands to actually marching, or the idea of watching (and listening to) the other bands, so I guess he didn't really care about pretending otherwise.

Seeing the unconvinced look on the section leader's face, I guess I felt that it would be more awkward to feign agreement with Wes than to just answer myself. My mouth faster than my brain, as was typical on the occasions I actually opened it, I blurted out something like "actually, I'm pretty damn nervous". She laughed, letting me know that it was no big deal, and that it would be even easier "next time". Turning red, I replied that I didn't think there was going to be a next time. I'm not sure what made me answer at all. I guess it felt like a chance to tell someone the truth.

"What?!" she asked, a genuinely incredulous look on her face. I stuttered my way through a response, rambling something unintelligible about how I couldn't perform in front of so many people, and I could hardly even talk to one person like I was trying to right now, and I didn't enjoy it anyway, and I didn't even know why I had joined in the first place. I don't remember exactly what she said in response; I was just staring at the ground, wishing I was anywhere else. I remember hearing sympathy in her tone, and yet feeling unheard by her knowing words: something to the effect of "give it a chance".

It really began to set in that, for most people, anxiety was a rare sensation, one more of confusion than anything else, and would fade away with nothing more than time. Well, I'd given it a chance, and nothing had changed. I realized that talking to others about my anxiety was just opening myself up to personal humiliation—to a reminder that I was a coward for not facing my fears, or else that I was abnormal; broken.

She and Wes paced around and talked to others in the line. I stood quietly, face still burning, until it was finally time to enter the stadium. I hardly remember our performance. I stared out vacantly as the other bands marched, occasionally responding to Wes or Chris walking up to talk. It was at least evening now, and I hadn't eaten all day; I had the money to buy something from whoever was selling food at the event, but not the ounce of courage I needed to approach them. When Wes finally decided to get some food, I gave him some money and asked him to get me something, pretending I was too lazy to walk over to the line.

After the competition, only the hometown holiday parade remained—horrible, due to everyone watching, but at least mercifully brief in comparison—and then my time in marching band was over. There would be an optional trip at the end of the next semester which involved performing and hanging out at some theme park, and Wes did want me to come—but this time, I stuck to what I believed was best for me, and I didn't sign up.

The holiday break at the end of the calendar year hadn't been something I had particularly looked forward to, not since I was six years old or so. My parents used it as an opportunity to argue over which one of them would get to see us on Christmas Day, and which would have to settle for Christmas Eve, as if it actually made a difference. By this time in my freshman year, myself and my siblings were all quite sure that we were not, in fact, Christians like our parents, but each somewhere between agnostic and atheist. Mom found our lack of faith to be abhorrent, and at this time of the year especially, she liked to remind us that she didn't want us to go to hell. I have very few memories of these holidays, and that year's is no exception. I mainly remember the relief of marching band being over: a feeling so freeing, it was as if I had survived a terminal illness.

THE VALLEY OF SELF-DOUBT

As school picked back up in January, so did my anxiety—not to the level it had been during marching band, but notably higher than before. I no longer had near-weekly embarrassments looming on the horizon, but many anxious sensations lingered: feelings that everyone's eyes were on me; feelings that I was constantly revealing myself to them to be stupid, impotent, childish, or laughable. Everyone seemed to expect that, after I had just given new, uncomfortable things a chance, they'd be easier. On the contrary, exposing myself to that fear seemed, even after it was over, to have made my entire life more miserable.

I was still in symphonic band, having signed up for it at the beginning of the year. Just holding my saxophone magnified my lingering anxieties, and I really couldn't enjoy playing the instrument anymore. Since I enjoyed the thought of talking to the school administrators about a schedule change even less, I decided I could make it through one more concert. The music was much more difficult than what I'd played before, and I didn't have it in me to practice outside of class, so I just moved my fingers vaguely along to certain parts without playing. The band director caught on to this, giving me looks of skepticism and irritation, but never saying anything.

I floated vacantly through the semester, not really noticing or caring about much, other than avoiding anxiety. I might not have said that I was unhappy, exactly; I still played with my own band, played my new favorite video game, *Dark Souls*, with James, Chris, and my brother, and didn't have any standout moments of humiliation—but I was just going through the motions. A lot of people describe depression as feeling like that. To me, in the years since that time, depression has seemed like more than that—like a feeling of visceral, irreparable despair. I guess it was just beginning to set in at the time.

Most of my memories of the time are of fleeting moments, but one thing that happened stood out above all others. A boy in my grade took his own life. An administrator announced his passing over the intercom during our first period, followed by a minute of silence. The first thing to strike me was a chilling confusion. I had been in classes with him since middle school, and we had spoken a couple times. I barely knew him, but I knew his confident smirk, and his unreserved attitude. I couldn't believe that a guy like him had made a choice like that. Then again, at the time, I couldn't believe that anyone would even think about suicide. Through all the discomfort and fear I had felt, I had never truly thought that I needed to let go of it all.

The second thing that struck me was how much more everyone seemed to care about him, now that he was gone. It didn't surprise me to see his best friend crying. It wasn't weird that some people that weren't very close to him were still very upset, on principle. What was strange was that, suddenly, it seemed that everyone knew him so well, and missed him so deeply. He had been of fairly average popularity, and yet now, everyone spoke as if he had been their best friend. Did people just feel the need to express their general sadness in a way that felt personal? Or, had he genuinely affected so many people in ways that perhaps neither they, nor he, had realized until he was gone?

These thoughts would stick with me well past the end of my first year of high school, which itself was heralded by an award ceremony. I was familiar with that sort of event, the same thing having happened throughout middle school, and was generally not a fan of them. On one hand, it was nice to hear from someone, in this case a teacher, that they thought I'd done a good job. It wasn't something I heard a whole lot, except when doing something my parents were specifically interested in. Having largely quit making attempts to fish or hunt with my dad, finding his hobbies not to my sensibilities, and now having performed saxophone for my mom for the last time, compliments would mean even more to me when I could get them.

On the other, much larger hand, such events were nerve-wracking for me. For one thing, you didn't get to know ahead of time which awards you would have to walk across the stage to receive, so you just had to listen for your name. At least I am lucky to have a very simple name to pronounce; some of my classmates could hardly tell when they were being called, due to whoever was reading the student list absolutely massacring their names. Unfortunately, my name does fall at the end of the alphabet, meaning that I would probably be the last person to trip their way across the stage, after anxiously listening to however many other names being called (something like a grade-point average award entailed a long list).

That sort of anxiety had been there since sixth grade. But now, I especially hated how guilty the whole concept of the event made me feel. What did I do in a required-credit high school class that was so special that I deserved an award, even one printed on cardstock? I was just doing what I had to do. There was nothing impressive about me: I wasn't able to be the fun guy in the stands at football games, or to even play all my parts right at a concert, or to so much as stay awake and pay attention in class. It kind of felt egotistical to feel good about myself. More than that, our first period teachers had to hand out invitations to anyone who'd gotten an award, making anyone who hadn't received one feel conspicuously excluded. It was nice when someone made me feel good about achieving my own goals, but I hated feeling like I was being labeled as somehow "better" than someone else.

I got quite a few of these awards throughout middle and high school, but I only really remember one, and it was from that ninth-grade year. They had gotten through the general academic awards, and began the awards for specific classes. I zoned out at this point, confident that, while I had done alright in my classes, these sorts of awards went to students that actually participated. Eventually, they started going through elective classes, the presenter running through them at a rate that suggested it was past his bedtime. I hadn't realized those would be included. Maybe I'd get an award for being the kid that walked the most laps around in the gym in second semester P.E., instead of participating in any of the other activities.

Then, my web design teacher walked on the stage. After a very brief introduction, the presenter called my name. It took me a second to register what was happening, before Wes helpfully said "That's you!" and ejected me from my seat. I half-jogged up to the stage, tripping on the stairs for at least the second time that night, and got a smile, a handshake, and a piece of paper from my favorite teacher. It's strange how, even when it feels like nothing really matters that much, a small sign—that somebody noticed you, and saw just a bit of what you want to be showing through—can mean everything.

As another summer began, I had just turned 15, which meant that I was old enough, where I lived, to get a learner's permit. This would allow me to drive a car, while an adult with a license was a passenger, and to get an actual license once I was 16. I was extremely anxious, and not particularly excited by the prospect, as I had no interest in going anywhere, except where I absolutely had to. However, my sister would be graduating after next year, and my brother would be starting high school the semester after that. I was expected to drive him, and myself, to and from school, if nothing else. To get the standard license upon turning 16, the learner in question had to pass a driving test, but first had to have their parents or instructor sign off on having participated in a certain minimum of practice-driving hours. My parents had each individually participated in a roughly equal amount of hours with my sister, after which my mom made clear that she would not be highly involved in attempting to teach me or my brother.

So Dad would be my sole mentor. He attempted to remain calm and encouraging for about five minutes, while I turned on the car, tried to remember which pedal was which, and worked the gear shift. Then, I drove a little bit on the driveway, discovering that the steering wheel in his ancient SUV had what felt like a deadzone, which would have been difficult enough for someone who could already drive to have compensated for. Next, I learned that looking backwards to reverse made me extremely dizzy and nauseous; as I stopped the car and announced this, I could already hear any patience Dad might have had being replaced by tension in his clipped response.

Well, we wouldn't have to reverse on the rural highway just off the driveway, so there we proceeded. Already extremely anxious at the prospect of dealing with other drivers, at the same time as my own poor hand-eye coordination, I panicked and floored the gas pedal as I entered the highway. The old SUV didn't exactly have the acceleration of a sports car, but you could feel it jump. Dad immediately snapped, turning and bellowing in my ear a command to slow down. I leveled out at about ten miles under the speed limit, apologizing in a shaky voice as I tried to keep my composure. Seconds later, a pickup truck was riding my tail; I hadn't checked my mirrors yet to notice its approach.

"Somebody's right on you, gotta speed up now!" Dad shouted, sounding as if his jaw was clenched. I yelled something sarcastic in response as I attempted to ease onto the gas pedal. The truck passed me, going ten or fifteen miles above the speed limit. I stared at the road, trying to ignore my dad rapidly turning his head between the road and myself. "Stay in your lane!" he yelled. I had slightly crossed the centerline, and there was someone coming now in the other lane. Clenching the wheel, I overcorrected. "Stay on the goddamn road, Jacob!" he screamed in amendment to his previous sentiment, as I nearly missed a mailbox.

All forty or more hours of practicing driving went like this to some degree, an anxiety that dominated my summer and persisted in the months to follow. Of course, I improved significantly, but it didn't feel like that—it only meant longer moments of tense silence to look forward to, before it was broken by a shouted reprimand for whatever mistake I had made. It made me act extremely paranoid, and feel like I was too stupid to learn something that everyone else did.

But I knew it wasn't specific to learning to drive—it was just me. I did alright academically, but I'd learned that that was the bare minimum for everyone. I was decent at playing saxophone, but I had given up on that now, and besides, music wouldn't help me succeed in life, so it didn't really matter. Everything else my parents had tried to teach me, I was terrible at. If I was doing anything right, surely they would have told me? If I hadn't been uniquely unable, surely they wouldn't have gotten so angry at me? If I had even had the capability to learn and improve, I knew they wouldn't have given up on me at the earliest opportunity. Or maybe it was like they said—I wasn't stupid, I just wasn't trying, because I was lazy and didn't care enough.

Mom had always told me that Dad was mean and manipulative, and I shouldn't listen to him. Dad had always told me that Mom was unreasonable and unstable, and I shouldn't listen to her. But, when I first drove with my mom as a passenger, after having improved significantly, I knew that they were in agreement about one thing—that I was a terrible driver. She clearly felt terrified, and acted hypervigilant, and squealed commands, certain I was not managing on my own. So I couldn't dismiss her as being "unreasonable", nor Dad as having been "mean"; their reactions showed that they both agreed, so it seemed like they were both right. I couldn't learn how to do this simple thing that everyone else did, and whether it was because I was stupid, or lazy, or some combination or the two, I couldn't seem to do anything about it.

Now, at least sometimes, I know that none of that was true. Neither of them had ever tried to teach me in the first place, the right way to drive, or to do anything else; they had simply demanded that I learn. They never explained why the mistakes I made were incorrect, or how I could fix or avoid them. The best feedback I could ever hope to receive was some small hint of my error, obscured within their frustrated vocalizations. Even the smartest person trying their hardest to learn makes mistakes, but my parents had no patience nor desire to teach me; they just wanted me to learn, so that I could take some of the burden my existence had caused them off of their own shoulders.

brother and sister, in the ways I could only dream they would to me. It would be nice right now to hear nothing; to feel nothing; to rest. I just kept restarting the video, considering this realization. Eventually, I turned it off and passed out, eyes still wet. The feeling that I needed to die mostly went away by the next morning, but now it was not shy about coming back from time to time; contemplating, after each occasion, whether it would be staying for good this time.

There's still a big difference between being unable to see your own worth—to find your own happiness—and truly hating yourself. Now that I've felt both feelings, I can see that difference in myself, at different points. As my sophomore year of high school began, I began to feel like I was inferior to others—my parents, my siblings, my classmates—but I almost didn't care. I knew what expectations people had of me. I felt like I had never met any of them, and I knew that trying to just reminded me how worthless I was. Now, I made the unconscious decision that I wasn't going to try any more, not for anyone else. I was going to do whatever made me comfortable at any given moment, avoid thinking about whatever anyone (including myself) expected of me, and live whatever life I ended up with.

Constantly sleeping in class, rather than trying to pay attention to the statistics teacher, after a night with maybe four hours of stressed sleep, became comfortable quite quickly. Utterly failing assignments that didn't count much towards my grade, then figuring out what I was supposed to have already learned when we went over the answers, was a surprisingly reliable way to just barely get A's on important tests. The one thing that I really had the energy to care about was avoidance: preventing others from reinforcing how bad I felt about myself. Soon, I learned that if I made fun of myself first—consistently—no one else would ever have a chance. Besides, if I was the one saying it, I could always tell myself it was just a joke.

My personality changed a lot, in a short period of time. In getting creative with my self-deprecation, I became adept at sarcasm. Soon, its use was my main conversational strategy. There's almost always an easy place to insert sarcasm in a conversation, and doing so allowed me to participate, and make people laugh, all without drawing any attention to the parts of me I wasn't comfortable sharing—my interests, my emotions, or really anything more than my raised eyebrows and vacuous humor. It had the additional benefit of hamstringing the conversation, keeping it as the sort of pointless back-and-forth that was easier to handle than anything meaningful. Expletives also began to dominate my vocabulary, as I figured out that they gave me an easy way to convey strong—albeit simplistic—emotions. I felt like I faced less risk of embarrassment by acting needlessly coarse than I would have, if I had tried to convey emotion openly and honestly.

Whatever sort of social life I had continued to shrink. Wes only ended up in one class with me that year, and we pretty much only spoke when he randomly dropped by where James and I were sitting, in the morning before classes. Neither of us ever said anything about it, but I think he could feel, as I did, that our friendship was gradually ending. We didn't have any issues with each other; we were just heading in different directions. Wes was starting to get his shit together, and as it turns out, I was beginning to lose mine. And, only a couple months into the year, my own band fell apart, as Will, the guitarist from the grade above me, eventually just stopped responding to messages about scheduling practices. It was frustrating to have it end like that, but I was mostly relieved that someone, somehow, had made their intentions clear, and it was over.

The second semester began, and with it, one class I was actually looking forward to: AP Computer Science. I didn't know exactly what we were going to cover, but ever since I had started learning to program in middle school, I had known that I was going to have a career in game development, and I had continued to learn in my free time. Finally, I could be more than self-taught, figure out whether I had actually learned anything useful, and earn a college credit towards something I actually cared about.

As it turned out, it was taught by the AP Calculus teacher, who was quite old, not quite as much of a programmer as I had hoped for from a college-level course, and, in fact, retiring at the end of the year. On the first day, we went through the list of topics that we'd need to understand for the College Board test, and I was disappointed to realize that, though the language we'd be programming in was not one I'd learned, I was already familiar with all of it. Considering I'd been learning for three-and-a-half years, I shouldn't have been surprised, but I guess I wasn't giving myself much credit.

In a move I imagine she regretted deeply, our teacher allowed those of us that had our own laptops to bring and use them instead of the school's, at my request. I had asked with good intentions: I wanted to set up the development software on my own computer, so I could keep using it at home. I was not ignorant to the fact that my oversized gaming laptop, which might as well have been a desktop for its pitiful battery life, was a potential distraction. However, I did underestimate its impact, as everyone within a 2-desk radius immediately demanded to know what video games I had installed. I may have, to some degree, been responsible for five-sixths of the class playing a massive *Halo* match on more than one occasion. In my defense, our teacher generally passed out an assignment and then sat silently at her desk, while everyone attempted to figure out how to do it on their own. I don't think I'd be exaggerating to say I, along with one other student, put as much time into teaching other students how to program as she did.

In the time since then, I've often thought back on my sophomore year, and felt that I was the happiest I've ever been. Relatively speaking, I didn't much care what anyone else thought of me, as long as they didn't get a chance to tell me. I spent my free time immersing myself in the things that calmed me, rather than engulfing myself in the distressing inclinations of others. I let myself be whatever came comfortably.

Only now do I know that I wasn't really comfortable; I was only limiting my discomfort. I wasn't doing things that made me happy, just avoiding things that made me anxious. I cared less about what others thought of me, not because of some healthy realization, but because I didn't care about what I thought about myself. I didn't see things to hate about myself, but I didn't see any worth in myself, either.

There was nothing there to care about. That was freeing, in a way. My happiness then was real, but it was only relative, and it couldn't last. I didn't much care where my life went, but it was inevitably going to go somewhere, and I'd be dragged along with it. At some point, I'd be forced to either give up entirely, or start caring.

One morning in April, our computer science teacher announced that the school was looking for a student, heading into their junior or senior year, to work as an assistant to the technology department—specifically, to the person working under the lengthy title of Technology Support Technician (referred to with the acronym TST). Apparently, each of the high schools in the county where I lived always had one or two of these assistants—usually one outgoing, one incoming—and as one of ours would be graduating this year, they were hiring another. Whoever was hired would be working over the summer around the school system, and throughout the school next year in lieu of one class period, and surprisingly, they would actually be paid.

An opportunity more suited to myself at the time could not have existed. Everything it would entail overwhelmed me with anxiety: giving up the few months of time alone between school years; replacing it with driving around to places I hadn't been before; and working cooperatively with others, rather than doing what needed to be done on my own. But I could do work that I was familiar with, and at least somewhat interested in; I could show my parents that I was worth something, even if only minimum wage; and I could prove to myself that I could care about something, if I wanted to, while also having one less pointless class to pretend to care about. If my career was going to be my life, it was time to learn what that meant.

I was one of only two students that ended up applying. The other was an acquaintance of mine since elementary school, who was just as qualified as me. However, my appearance better fit the stereotype of a relatively-kempt nerd, and since I had the charisma of a pebble in an earthquake, I'm assuming my haircut was the primary factor in their decision to hire me. That decision came after a nerve-wracking interview, which, though quite simple and surface-level by the standards of actual job interviews, nonetheless involved three or four people staring me down while I stuttered at them, and wondered how I could convince all of these smart, important people that I could handle the job, when I hardly trusted myself to do anything right. I left feeling like I had only succeeded in humiliating myself, but that ended up being sufficient to get the spot.

I had a couple weeks off at the end of May, before it was time to return to school as an employee, but had to use the time to practice for my driving test. It turned out to make little difference. It took me multiple minutes to successfully parallel park, even though I had gotten pretty fast at it while practicing, and I backed over more than one cone while reversing. Somewhat terrifyingly, they still considered this performance sufficient to earn a driver's license, and I was now legally capable of working my first job.

My first day arrived, and I headed to the high school, anxiety in tow. A man that I'd met briefly during the interview waved me over and re-introduced himself; he would be my supervisor around the county for the summer, and I would work with the TST only during the school year. He gave me his number, then texted the others irritably to ask where they were (jokingly so, as I was about 20 minutes early). While we waited for them to arrive on time, he explained more specifically what we'd be doing over the summer: put simply, installing some new stuff, and making sure the old stuff worked as expected.

We poked around some computer labs, and I learned where various tools and cables were stashed in his van, before the others showed up. The two of them, one having just graduated from my school, and the second a rising senior at the other high school, each seemed evidently more intelligent and ambitious than myself, through the distorted lens of my nonexistent self-esteem. Hopefully, I would be presented with limited opportunities to make myself look like an idiot.

Fortunately, I had a pretty good idea of what I was doing, and things went smoothly for the most part. There were very few staff around the schools on most days, which was a huge relief; I talked to very few people, other than those I'd met on the first day, who were thankfully all kind and funny. More than anything, everyone was very patient with me—I think it was obvious I was extremely anxious, and they did a lot to make it easier for me without any complaint. I never really got comfortable with it—there could always be a surprise that I wasn't prepared to handle (and there were), or I might get lost driving to a school I had already worked at a few times (and I did), and that was on top of my baseline social anxiety—but I did it, and that was enough for the moment.

Since we were usually the only people around, one guy brought a Bluetooth speaker and streamed music off Spotify. Soon, the others started requesting the sort of stuff they liked, and we listened to a blend of rap, pop, and country. Inevitably, my supervisor asked what kind of music I liked. There was nothing I was less comfortable talking about than my taste in music. If I absolutely had to talk about something I liked, I could talk about video games—most of the time, people wouldn't know enough about them to continue the conversation, and if they did, it was probably because they had similar tastes to me.

But music is too universal—everyone knows the major genres, or at least they think they do. Even talking about myself was easier, now; my constant self-deprecating jokes were very handy for preventing other people from teasing me in ways that would cut deeper than they knew. Unfortunately, that doesn't work as well for your interests—I am who I am, whether I like it or not, but my interests are things I've already decided I like. Talking about them would always leave me open to being judged for them.

"I'm good with whatever you guys want to listen to," I responded to my supervisor's question. In a misguided but kind attempt at making me feel comfortable requesting something I liked, he kept prodding. He knew I had played saxophone in band; perhaps I liked classical music. Not particularly, I said, but I didn't mind it. Maybe jazz? Certainly Kenny G. Both were fine, I told him. Then, he said, I seemed like the rocker type. Supposing that he was going to go through every genre one-by-one until he guessed right, I told him he was getting warmer. My face was getting warmer, too. Usually the heavier stuff, I admitted, hoping he would be deterred and drop it. That sounded to him like what his son (also in my class) liked. Maybe he'd know about something specific that I liked?

Usually metal, I said, insisting that they wouldn't like it, and that the low notes wouldn't sound very good on the Bluetooth speaker, and that I'd rather just listen to what they liked. That still didn't end it; everyone's questions slowly tapered off throughout the day as I continually refused to give them anything else to work with. It was extremely embarrassing; I had completely failed to pull off the "I like all kinds of music" vibe, because I'm not a very good liar, and they simply didn't understand why I wouldn't be comfortable just listening to music I liked. I wouldn't have even been comfortable playing something in a genre I knew they all liked—just in case they didn't like one band in particular—much less the new Mastodon album. I had seen not only instant, visceral reactions of disgust people had to the things I liked, especially heavy music, but also how what they thought about me as a person had changed from then on.

With the school year almost upon us, the actual amount of work we had to do mostly tapered off—other than one sudden, frenzied installation of a late batch of new computers—and yet the job became far more difficult for me, as staff began to return for preplanning at all of the schools. From the administrators that were irritated that we weren't out of their way yet, to the teachers that wanted to make small talk about how their new "computer" (monitor) was half-an-inch wider, I was constantly walking around with my jaw clenched in dread. And this, I realized, was nothing, compared to all the people that would be in the school during the year. My ninety minutes of work each day would feel like an eternity compared to these fleeting five hours.

My sister was now moving out of our parents' houses, and into her college dorm. I was jealous, not because I was looking forward to college, and obviously not that the idea of sharing a small room with someone else appealed to me, but because I was not looking forward to another two years of being passed between my parents.

It seemed like my dad rarely spoke to me without first an exasperated sigh, regretful and tired of the life he'd trapped himself in, and I could only hope I wouldn't mess something up, or ask a question he thought I should know the answer to, and provoke his ire. I couldn't be around my mom without being made to feel guilty, whether because she claimed that we kids loved my dad more than her, or because we hadn't cared about her enough to spend time doing the things she wanted, or shown her enough emotive appreciation at the right moments, or because one of us had failed in our attempt to stoically reassure her away from her overwhelming negative emotions, and had shown some emotion ourselves. If I ever smiled or laughed around her, she assumed it was because I was making fun of her; I caught myself stifling any signs of happiness when I was around others, or even completely alone. I tried to ignore as they each lambasted me about the problems they each continued to cause each other, as if I was responsible for them.

They didn't seem to see me as an individual, nor notice my constant anxiety, even on the occasions I broke down before them; they saw a child, their child, meant to do as he was told—physically, mentally, and emotionally. That was the one thing that they could agree on: that, while they each loved me, and they knew the other did, they loved me as their child, and never, in any capacity, as an emotional equal. Many times, my sister went through so much, mediating the anger while my brother and I fled to our rooms. Now, she left, as she deserved to do. I was the oldest child left. Without any reassurance that I was capable, and plenty of the opposite, I was to be the responsible one for my brother, and the emotional outlet for my parents.

NOTHING I COULD DO

My job resumed on the first day of junior year, replacing my third class period. I approached the office of the person I'd be assisting, the TST, trying to remind myself that the work over the summer could have been much worse than it was. The TST greeted me energetically, and we had an introductory conversation for a few minutes, which got progressively more uncomfortable for each of us. It became clear that she was that cheery, outgoing sort of person for whom nothing was too boring to talk about, social anxiety was a foreign concept, and emotional reservation was a sign of conscious apathy, demonstrated by rude people. As it dawned on her that I was this sort of reserved person, she set me on a task without much further delay.

All the ways I had imagined the summer work having been potentially worse were quickly realized. Most of my assignments entailed walking halfway around the school, to a certain classroom or computer lab. Teachers I passed along the way eyed me warily from within their rooms; students I knew, and some I didn't, en route to or from a bathroom, wanted to know where I was going with that Ethernet cable during class time. When I reached my destination, the teacher in the room was often surprised by my presence, having expected the TST to come herself, or not having realized that anyone was coming, to do anything with their technology.

There was generally a full class in the room, guaranteeing me stares, whispers, and snickers from other kids—the sort of thing most people would respond to with some silly gesture of their own, or ignore entirely, or perhaps never even notice. On many occasions, a teacher would be actively giving a lesson, and I'd have to try to find a good moment to interrupt, awkwardly approaching and clearing my throat, receiving audible comments and giggles from the class. The same sort of thing continued as I did whatever I was supposed to be doing. Usually, "the computer wouldn't come on", which meant that I had to crawl under their desk to discover that they'd unplugged their monitor with their foot. I'd see their exasperation at me as I had to ask them to move away from the computer so I had room to work. Some stared suspicious holes into the back of my head, as if I were going to steal the sticky notes off their desk.

The job was so simple, and yet so unbelievably difficult for me. The first half of each day, I couldn't think about anything but that office; the person in it, who seemed off-put by my mere presence; the teachers that seemed to have no trust or patience to spare me; and the kids that seemed to see me as a clumsy, laughable, groveling nerd. Every day, I'd sweat, stutter, and shake my way through the simplest tasks, only seeming to inflame the signs of others' disgust in me. I was often too nauseous to eat at all during the day, until it was over, when I'd try to find a few minutes to wolf something down on the way to my last class. It didn't help that my best friend, James, attended school online only this semester, as he was having a very hard time with narcolepsy. The best part of each day was when I was just stewing in the shame I'd caused myself that day, before the dread returned in preparation for the next. I truly hated it—I hated that I couldn't handle something so easy; something that, to some degree, I actually wanted to do; something that, for once, I chose to try, all on my own.

In my opinion, these experiences were the beginning stages of avoidant personality disorder. What had been a simple social anxiety, an instinctual fear of the unknown, had evolved with what I'd experienced. I had learned how to be a good person, but not how to be myself in the meanwhile. I hadn't figured out how to express emotions, but had discovered that it was safer to do the opposite. I had realized how behind I was in these things that other people saw as normal, and noticed that I made people uncomfortable by failing to meet their emotional expectations. I had seen patterns in the subtle signs of others' discomfort, and became preoccupied with watching for them to appear again. I would dread the things I knew would come, as if dwelling on the fear would allow me to find a solution; I would panic when these objects of my dread arrived, as I went into overdrive trying to relieve myself and others of my own tangible anxiety; and I would forever feel the shame for my failure to do so: an admonition upon myself, for having let myself end up in such a scenario, in which I was doomed to fail not just myself, but everyone else.

Even as horrible as marching band had been, it wasn't the same as this. I had no faith in my ability to perform in those shows—but I still had faith in myself. I knew I was trying to be a good friend to Wes by even doing it; I was trying to do a decent job for the sake of it, despite my total lack of interest. I was good at some things, good *for* some things—just not marching band. By the time I started working that year, that faith in myself was fading away. I had managed the summer job due to luck—there wasn't much interaction required of me, and the people I worked with often made an effort they didn't have to, in order to make me feel more comfortable.

Now, I would need more than luck, and I didn't have it. As I had learned to drive, and been made to feel like I was doing a terrible job of it, I began to feel that I just wasn't good at anything. I had looked back, finding patterns in my past, proving to myself that I never had been. I spent my sophomore year living this belief, simply uncaring of anything, not feeling up to trying. Now, I had felt the need to try once more, and I was failing once again. It felt like everyone was noticing. The kids in the classrooms seemed to mock me, though it's really more likely they were laughing about their teacher's reaction to me, or lack thereof. The teachers seemed angry at me, but they were probably just annoyed at their class getting derailed with little warning. Worst of all, the way my boss acted around me made me doubt whether I had ever really been, at the least, the nice, polite, and attentive person I thought I had.

Partly out of the understanding that this was the extreme low end of the sorts of adversity I'd have to deal with all the time as an adult, and a resultant desperation not to give up, and partly because I didn't want to humiliate myself more by trying to get out of my commitment, I made it through the semester. I tried to focus on my finals; work wasn't going to get any worse this close to the break, but my grades certainly still could. I had consistently slept my way through my morning classes in particular, including AP Calculus. While I had learned enough outside of class just before each test to do decently, I had forgotten it all immediately afterwards, with my mind elsewhere.

Any student that participated in the school's work program for a class period had to check in with its director occasionally. My last scheduled meeting with her arrived, and I assumed it would be the same sort of brief, pointless chat as the others. The first thirty seconds were the usual sort of pleasantries, during which I feigned only the mildest enthusiasm for my job; then, she handed me a manila envelope. Enclosed, she said, was a feedback sheet, which I was to provide to my boss to fill out about me, and which essentially governed my grade in the "class".

Then I was sent on my way, with the envelope, and with the most explicit realization I'd had yet that I really feared knowing what people thought about me. I worried more by the day about the mistakes I seemed to make, and the people that seemed to notice, and the ways they seemed to feel about me. I doubted myself with everything I did, but as long as no one said anything, doubts would remain doubts, and I could temper my shame. Now, I had to hand my boss the envelope, and ask her (in so many words) to say how she really felt. I hoped that I had just been too sensitive, and I was reading too much into it, and she liked me just fine. Maybe I would just receive a grade from the feedback, and I'd never even get to see it personally.

A couple weeks later, the last day arrived. With most teaching and testing over, there was little tech in need of fixing, so I stashed my stuff in the TST's office and hung out in the library about ten yards away. An hour-and-a-half later, it was over, at least for a few weeks, and I went back into the office to retrieve my belongings, and make an awkward attempt to earnestly bid my boss a merry Christmas. Within seconds, I was heading back out the door when she remembered: the work program director had wanted her to give me this. Of course it was that damn envelope. I thanked her as I took it, half-flinging the door open as I fled.

I had to open it. Maybe she gave me some constructive criticism that would really hurt, but might eventually help. I couldn't rule out the possibility that she'd said something really nice, and even though I was really terrible at showing it, the rare compliments I received made me feel giddy with happiness for hours. Even if she'd said the worst, I needed to know, in the same way that I had to be hypervigilant of peoples' reaction to me. I no longer had the option of doubting any feelings about what she thought about me—the truth was right there. To be able to shrug it off would have been the same as being able to take others' direct questions or criticisms of me with a grain of salt. It would have been a greatly freeing feeling which, by that point, I was completely incapable of having.

I got in my car in the school parking lot, knowing I'd be waiting fifteen minutes or so for my brother to show up. I pulled the sheet out of the envelope. I quickly looked through all the categories which she had been asked to offer feedback on. All the ones directly related to the work I was doing had her general approval, with no further comments. The last section was about me, specifically. Was I polite, accommodating, and a team player?

I saw the ink that would answer these questions in my peripheral vision, and my heart sank before I could read it. I thought of what my mom had said many times, more often now that I was the oldest child left to vent to—that I was short, uncaring, even mean. I thought of all the small signs everyone had always shown that I was making them uncomfortable with my words and mannerisms. I read the comment she had written in this section—the only full words written on the page.

"Needs to be more friendly." So few words, so non-specific, from someone whom I really barely knew, and they were burned into my mind. Passing words, that probably didn't mean much to her: someone who was just used to a more sociable type than myself, who thought I was choosing to be distant and cold out of a disregard or dislike for her; who thought I needed to know that I'd have to be more personable to expect anyone to hire me for a real job.

Those words meant everything to me. I stared at them for minutes, trying to accept the truth, of everything I had ever worried about myself. I felt sick, but I didn't feel like crying. I cried from sadness when a pet died; from guilt when I blamed myself for my

parents' emotions; from fear when they turned their
rage upon me; or from depression, when my
embarrassments were in the past rather than the
present, and I realized, again, that I wished I was dead.
I teared up when I felt like I was being humiliated, but I
never cried. I couldn't cry from shame, or I would have
never stopped.

I couldn't stop thinking about how it made me feel.
I attempted to casually bring it up to some of my
family, as if it were a funny thing to make small talk
about, just an afterthought; hoping for, but not really
expecting, any reassurance. My brother just rhetorically
asked why I'd care what my boss thought about me. My
parents, individually, quizzed me as to whether I'd been
rude to her, before noncommittally shrugging off the
subject. None of them said they thought, too, that I
needed to be more friendly—but none of them said
otherwise, either. My brain filled in the blanks.

The next semester, I still pushed through. It was
disconcerting to be around my boss after that. She, of
course, acted the same combination of cheery and
exasperated towards me. I wanted to be more friendly,
but I could only be quieter and more terse. With the
classes I was taking only being available at specific
times, just the last period of the day was open for work,
so now the dread encompassed the entire school day.
Constantly anxious, I autopiloted my way through the
semester, remembering little but a constant sick
feeling.

I continued working into the next summer, which,
while still an immediate improvement for the same
reasons as before, was worse than it had been. A year of
constant dread, tangible panic, and freshly shameful

memories, paired with those five words written by my boss, had validated my anxiety to me. I would always feel this terrible, and not for reasons imagined—the discomfort I had thought I caused others was real. The only way to fight it was to be someone whom I clearly wasn't—someone who felt farther out of reach every day. There was no one to offer me reassurance, to bring me back out of that belief. With every short conversation I had to have, I felt more sure about how everyone felt about me; felt more hatred in myself for how I knew it was my fault; and yet felt more powerless to just seem normal.

Senior year arrived—and with it, the realization that my life was, soon, no longer going to ride on someone else's rails. The time had come to decide which way I was going to go. The classes I had chosen made my schedule appear as if it had been randomly generated. On one hand, it included two art classes and an oceanography elective, all known for being ridiculously easy, and an English class far below the level I had usually been in, as well as my job. On the other hand, it included AP German, and therefore a ton of speaking in front of others in a foreign language, an AP Physics class which, only offered at the other school in the county, necessitated a daily bus ride for myself and three other students (including my friend Isaac), as well as two more levels of calculus, which would be taught remotely from the college I was tentatively planning to attend.

I knew I couldn't do it. I still wanted to get a Computer Science degree, and work as a game developer, but I already knew it wouldn't happen. I had only gotten more anxious, less confident, and less able to focus and try throughout high school. Why should I have expected that I could handle college? Even more laughable was the prospect of attending the one I theoretically wanted to, for what seemed like the best education and career prospects. It was over an hour from my small hometown, and in a major city. It might have been a good fit for the person I wanted to be, but that wasn't who I was.

I didn't have a better idea, or another idea at all, so these unrealistic aspirations remained my plan. I wasn't really lying to myself anymore; I was mostly hiding the reality of my inevitable failure from my parents. Their biggest disappointment would come to pass, but not yet. In the meantime, I continued outwardly as if I was confident in the path my life would follow. I applied to the college I "wanted" to attend—silently, all too aware of some much smarter people around me that were doing the same—and also to the nearby college which Isaac and James were considering attending, where my sister was currently a student.

I lasted a couple months more at my job, before I knew I couldn't take it anymore. I told my boss I'd be quitting at the end of the semester. I lied about the reason why, some bullshit about how busy I was getting ready for college, knowing she wouldn't understand the truth. To say this news annoyed her would be an understatement; she made routine, half-joking remarks about it for the rest of the semester, but I accepted the humiliation, knowing it would finally end soon. Dad kept questioning me about my decision, visibly frustrated and defeated. No matter how I tried to explain, he didn't understand, nor accept, the extent of my anxiety.

AP German could have been worse, mostly because the class size was so small that James, Isaac, and myself made up one-fourth of it. Of course, it was still constantly embarrassing for me. We frequently had group discussions over a particular subject, where the teacher would bring up something, anything, and ask for everyone's opinion on it. Fortunately, one of the more engaged students than myself always wanted to answer first; whenever it had to be my turn, I'd volunteer the German equivalent of "I agree with that", adding minimal elaboration at my teacher's prodding. She knew well by now how anxious I was, as I'd been in her classes for four years. Sometimes, she'd let it slide, and sometimes, she'd stop anyone else from answering, to clarify that Jake would be answering first this time, ensuring that my response would be particularly stuttered and nonsensical as I panicked.

I was completely checked out during physics class. During lab assignments, I would vacantly watch as Isaac and the other guy in my group did the work, myself having no idea what was going on. I managed to get a decent grade, through a combination of luck, and the calculus basics I happened to remember. My current calculus class was a different story. I sat in the back of the library with the one other student taking the class, staring absently at the tiny chalkboard rendered on the ancient monitor, failing to listen to the remote professor's crawling lecture, each voice and footstep in the library a freshly distracting anxiety.

Eventually, I just started muting the lesson, listening to music on my phone instead, just trying to drown out the people muttering nearby, who were wondering out loud what the nerds at the back were doing. My classmate eventually realized that my headphones weren't plugged into the computer, and I had to awkwardly try to explain to her that I couldn't concentrate, and I honestly had no idea what was going on, anyway. This was not a concept she seemed to be familiar with, as someone whom I knew to be both much smarter and harder-working than myself. She continued to exclaim excitedly when she got a test score back, and then eagerly ask how I had done; not with any air of superiority, just in a manner meant to offer interest and encouragement. She always seemed a little surprised and uncomfortable when I replied "well, I passed" or "well, I almost passed". I guess she was a little confused about how I had ended up in that class, and I wouldn't blame her.

She wasn't the only one. One day, during the second semester, I bumped into my previous calculus teacher on the way into the library. He asked how I was doing, and *what* I was doing going to the library during class time. Even he, one of the nicest and most patient teachers I had ever had, could not completely conceal his surprise when he learned what class I was in. He asked me how it was going, and he got more than he bargained for as an answer. I told him that, honestly, I was barely passing, and was extremely anxious about college, and was *a little bit* depressed. My eyes started watering, but I held back tears. He was overwhelmed, and clearly had no idea what to say—stumbling over something like "that's rough, man. Just gotta keep it up. Best of luck to you"—before he continued on his way. I felt terrible for dumping all of that on him; I hadn't meant to say anything like that. It all just spilled out, and I only felt worse for it afterwards.

My depression swelled over those last few months of high school, as I finally started to grasp what my life really was. I was going to try to suffer through college, struggle into a career, and survive through a lifetime of anxiety, and for what? The friends I had at school allowed me to laugh, to vent, and to feel like I knew someone kind of like me. I truly appreciated them putting up with me, and making me feel just a bit more comfortable when so often out of my element—but what did their friendships really mean to me, or mine to them? If I had to interact with people, it was infinitely better that they liked me, rather than the alternative; but if I stopped talking to people entirely, would I really miss my friends? Would they miss me?

What else was there to miss about other people? The idea of having a romantic relationship was just as unfathomable to me as it had been in middle school. Love felt like a lie: a pale facade, shared between two people who were physically attracted to each other, and then shared with their children; and it was one that was rarely maintained. I knew that most people didn't see it that way; it was real to them. I was jealous of them, but what did it matter if they were right, and love could be real? There was nothing for anyone to love about me.

So I would have plenty of alone time, then...and what would I do with myself? I had never liked too many different things, and it wasn't for lack of trying, especially now: I would spend hours poring over lists of idle interests, active hobbies, things that people liked collecting, places that people had enjoyed exploring. I didn't care for any of it. Those things I had occupied myself with, for so long now, took mere minutes to make me angry, sad, and tired. I wondered if maybe I had never really enjoyed any of it.

The more I thought about it, the more it made sense. I had started playing instruments mostly out of a feeling that I had to participate in some organized hobby. I kept it up, mostly because it was the one thing I was kind of good at; the one thing at least a little outwardly unique and impressive about me. Now I was too anxious to play for (or with) anyone, and too depressed to even play half-decently alone. Video games had been a brainless source of entertainment, and an asocial form of competition. Now, they weren't enough to distract me from my own thoughts, and even they felt like too much work. It seemed that I hadn't really ever liked anything; I had just tried to be interesting, and to feel diverted, while I waited for life to begin. Now I knew that there had never been any reason for any of it, even without considering my social ineptitude. This was life—there was nothing to look forward to. Had a divine being appeared before me to take all my anxiety away, it felt like it would have changed so little.

I had thought about suicide before. I had felt like I wanted to die. In times of extreme distress, I had even felt like I wished I had an easy way to make it happen myself. Now, these thoughts followed me everywhere. At least twice every week, I thought about how I could kill myself, right then. I knew I'd probably mess it up, and end up worse off, as it seemed like I did with everything else. I read about various methods, never finding anything that I could bring myself to try. I read a lot of other stuff, too: from people that had felt the same way I did; from people trying to promise that things would get better. I stared at the suicide hotline number, always at the top of the page when searching for things like this—thinking about how it could never help someone like me—and cried quietly, hoping no one would hear me.

My life continued around me, and soon, envelopes arrived from the colleges I had applied to. I opened them both, knowing that the letters inside could only make me feel worse, and read the contents. I had been accepted to my sister's college. My first choice had put me on a wait list, along with at least one other guy I knew, who probably had a more compelling application than myself. Well, that was that. Even though it made me feel terribly stupid, I expected that at this point, and it wasn't hard to just shrug it off to anyone that asked. I didn't have to lie when I said that I really didn't care.

When the time came to make a decision, I accepted admission to the school that had offered it. If I had anything to offer my own life, I would know by the end of the year. I had decided I needed to live in a dorm and get some space from my family, but I wasn't sure whom it would be with, since the rooms accommodated two, and I had two close friends planning to attend. Then, James told me that he wouldn't be going—maybe just doing some online classes somewhere—and it struck me that he was just as depressed as I was. Isaac and I signed up to room together.

The last month of high school was a free fall. I failed my calculus final just hard enough to bring my final grade down to a 69.4. I emailed my professor with a lackluster attempt at correcting my wrong answers, and begged him to increase my score on it by one point, so that I could pass the class. Assumedly out of pity, he obliged. I drifted through the end-of-year events: senior portraits, class photos, and a weird last-day trip to a nearby park. I wanted to skip my graduation and the accompanying embarrassment, and pick up my diploma later, but my parents insisted that I attend, and I was too tired to really argue.

But, finally, it was over. No matter how terrible life was from now on, it was in my hands. It was a feeling of immense anxiety and depressing resignation, more than of excitement and freedom. A couple months of this feeling over the summer were immediately validated, as I first drove onto college campus: looking for a spot in a packed parking garage; finding the building, the floor, and the small room which I would be sharing with someone else for at least a few months; meeting a bunch of random smiling faces during orientation; and trying to figure out where the hell all my classes were.

It was immediately very difficult for me to care about any of my classes. Even putting the distractions of depression and anxiety aside, nearly all of the subjects were the same sort of stuff I had taken in high school, as less than one-third of my credit hours throughout the entire four years would be related to my major of Computer Science. The only such class I had now was one on basic logic, which was required for the degree. The curriculum included no programming; instead, we would discuss things like logical operators, which, other than already being familiar to most anyone with an interest in Computer Science, could have been more easily demonstrated by actually writing code rather than abstracting it. It didn't seem like the sort of course that had enough material to justify its own existence. Other classes included yet more biology, U.S. politics, world history, and one that was literally called "WALKING 1000" on my schedule.

Of course, it was impossible to consider them in a vacuum and ignore my mental health. I faced the same anxieties in each class as I had since middle school, except now I was up against higher expectations. Professors and classmates alike assumed that anyone who had made it to college was somewhat sociable, and would be skilled in the ability to focus on their work and put aside other concerns.

I was frequently required to work with the same group of students on relatively small out-of-class assignments for my biology course. I remember the confused, irritated looks on their faces the first time I had to awkwardly speak to them, as if it dumbfounded and offended them each personally, that someone like me was here, wasting their time; they instantly formed the opinion that I would make no effort on anything, and would assign me an insignificant slice of whatever we were supposed to be completing. They did not deliberately act condescending, and yet I felt like I was seen as no more than an obstacle to their success. It was humiliating just to have to sit next to them.

I faced similar issues in other classes, but of course, anxiety did not end when my lessons did. Just returning to my dorm room was a sickening process— worrying that I'd lose my keycard, or have to feel someone's eyes boring into my back as I fumbled to get it scanned; analyzing the probabilities of whether I'd have more uncomfortable encounters going up in an elevator this time, or on the stairs; hoping that no one would try to talk to me as I hastily jammed my key into our door.

I had to use the shared showers; extreme self-consciousness meant that I was extremely paranoid about anyone so much as glimpsing me without a shirt on. And, for whatever reason, it seemed a common occurrence for some guy to get bored while they were showering, and try to have a chat with anyone else that might be in the bathroom. I tried to wash at the most unusual times, but it helped little, and I often just put it off much longer than was advisable.

I did the same with meals, as much as possible. Going to the dining hall was possibly the worst part of it all. Everyone was in such a casual mood; eyes looked in all directions; people talked and laughed loudly and comfortably. After the first week, I had decided that I would not bother going, except when Isaac invited me to join him for dinner. Even then, I rarely ate much, not wanting anyone to see me go through a buffet line more than once, worried about being seen as a glutton, in spite of being skinny and continuing to lose weight. I visited my parents on the weekends, and grabbed some snacks, which became my primary source of calories.

Before college, I usually slept with relative success for about six hours, after a couple of trying, and would manage about four on an especially bad night. Now, I was lucky to get four. The anxiety of everything else would have made it difficult enough, but of course, I was now also sharing a room with someone else. It hardly mattered that he had been my friend for six years; I was constantly on edge. And, like most adults, he didn't sleep with a light on; so, neither did I, which meant that my nighttime vertigo returned.

I developed the habit of blaring loud music in my

headphones until I finally fell unconscious. Much like sleeping with lights in your eyes, this would be unhelpful for most people. In my case, I found that it seemed to make my anxious feelings seem more natural, and slowly shove aside the real reasons for my stress, until it was eventually all drowned out.

I didn't want to give up, like I always had, but I was breaking down. Suicidal thoughts were overwhelming me, and I didn't even have the privacy to cry. I decided to ask for help for once. I needed to see a mental health doctor, but I couldn't manage it. Instead, I asked my dad to see if a general doctor friend of his whom I already knew could help. I started a prescription depression medication, knowing it would take a long time to start working, and just trying to keep going.

Something was bound to break what little will I had left to try. It did not take long to discover what was going to do the trick. My schedule had ended up in such a way that, literally five minutes after one class, I was expected at another, on the complete opposite side of the campus. The distance was such that I could not have even been on time by taking the campus bus; even if a bus had been waiting for me, and taken me directly there with no stops in between, I would have been late. Of course, the buses actually showed up at random intervals, and stopped constantly along the way, and the possibility of taking one overlooked the reality that I was far too anxious to ever get on in the first place.

The first week or so, I speedwalked to the class, plenty embarrassed by the reactions I received to my tardiness. One day, the teacher lost any semblance of patience, and demanded that I stop being late. I explained the physical impossibility of my situation to her. She used the opportunity to remind me that I was an adult now, and that the problem was therefore mine alone. A few of the older students found that quite amusing.

That hour of embarrassment was the last one I suffered in that class. All I was accomplishing, by trying my hardest to make it, was pissing people off and humiliating myself, so I just stopped going. Isaac caught on to the fact that I seemed to suddenly have one less class on my schedule, so I had to tell him what happened, passing it as something funny, shrugging it off as if it didn't matter to me. I don't think he bought the act. I stared blankly at my laptop that time each day, trying to forget about what I wasn't doing.

But I couldn't. The shame consumed me. Sure, it was just one class, but I was going to have to get that credit eventually, and if not now, when? Eventually, I accepted the answer I already knew: I was never going to get it. I had failed earlier than I had imagined, but I had known it was going to happen sooner or later. Next, I stopped going to my biology class, knowing my group would have an easier time not having to deal with me. Then came my logic class; time to stop pretending I was going to get a Computer Science degree. I stuck with the world history course for longer, because Isaac was in it, but I couldn't try on any assignments.

Eventually, all that was left was a class about walking. I would have stopped bothering with it, except I knew I was driving Isaac up a wall by lying in our dorm room the whole day. Thankfully, since the class consisted entirely of walking circles around a gym for just under an hour, I managed it. I listened to the entirety of the album *California* by Mr. Bungle each time, finding the combination of a routine, and the absurdity of the genre-bending music, to be somehow soothing.

The prescription I was taking had absolutely no effect over the months, which, of course, only made me feel more terrible. I had known it might take some guesswork to find something that worked, so I tried to hold out hope as I began a different one. It took all I had not to drop out right then—to just keep living. I told myself I was staying so that Isaac wouldn't have to find a new roommate yet. Each time my parents asked how I was, and I told them I was the same as ever, they'd ask if I was remembering to take my pills. Each time I had to insist that I was really taking them, I would wonder if I was somehow doing something wrong with them; perhaps I had completely lost my shit, and I wasn't actually taking them at all.

Then, finally, something changed—unfortunately, for the worse. As with most prescriptions, the manufacturer listed for this one a litany of common possible side effects, which could occur even without the medication actually doing what it was intended to do. In this case, the wheel of misfortune landed on male sexual dysfunction. I kept taking it anyway, hoping that the side effects had decided to kick in a bit before the desired effects began.

Weeks more went by, with nothing but walking and waiting. Most of the time, my social anxiety lay dormant, in the form of dread. I offered it as little room to thrive as I possibly could, even rejecting most of Isaac's offers to go eat. One evening, I was in a slightly better mood, and was talking to Isaac about a video game or something. Before I really realized what I was doing, I was following him to the dining hall. I'm not sure, but I feel like he specifically tried to make that happen, and it means a lot to me either way.

I quieted down as we headed through the dorm, hearing people's conversations in voices muffled by thin walls, and my anxiety began to seep in. It was already getting dark, though, and we probably wouldn't run into too many people on the way. Anyway, no one wanted to talk to me—I don't think I had ever run into someone I knew from high school other than Isaac, and it was past the part of the semester where the extroverts were trying to make any new friend they could. Unfortunately, the thing about crushing social anxiety is that you don't need bad luck to end up in an uncomfortable situation. What other people might call a cool coincidence, or just plain good luck, might make you feel sick and pathetic.

We walked out the door, and ran directly into someone I didn't think I would ever see again. "Hey, guys!" greeted the girl I had had a crush on since a seventh grade math class so long ago. She was with a friend of hers I didn't know, who continued into the dorm alone. I was paralyzed with panic. I made eye contact with her for a moment, before focusing my gaze on my feet. I have little idea of what happened after that. I think she greeted us both by name, because I remember vaguely feeling surprised that she remembered me. I probably plastered a closed-mouth smile on my face before freezing completely. She spoke to Isaac. I couldn't open my mouth. Then, she was gone.

We went on to the dining hall. I think Isaac asked if

I didn't recognize her, or why I didn't say anything, but maybe that recollection is just my own shame being personified. It wasn't so different from any of my other embarrassments, and maybe more minor. I'm sure neither she nor Isaac remembers it. Still, I'll never forget the specific sensation of shame, tinged with unconscious regret, and the wish that I had been anyone but myself in that moment.

SALVATION IN MY TRUTH

My medication never started working. After around ten weeks, I just stopped taking it. As the semester finally came to an end, I let Isaac know that I was dropping out, and he would need to find a new roommate. He appeared surprised, and asked why; I told him, at least a little bit, but I think he already knew. He just didn't know what he could say, and, of course, there was nothing he could have said. He texted me once, a few months later, about a video game. I answered halfheartedly. That was the last time we ever spoke.

I spent the next eighteen months doing almost literally nothing, in almost complete physical and mental isolation. It's not an exaggeration to say that I never went anywhere in public—I even learned to give myself haircuts. Outside of obligatory talks with family, I spoke to no one, other than to play a video game online with James sometimes. My anxiety was so complete that I'd refuse to even talk to him over the microphone, if my family was anywhere around. I rarely felt brave enough to post an anonymous comment about a video game on Reddit.

I had moved back in with my mom, shutting myself in my room as much as possible, just visiting my dad for dinner once a week. Their disappointment in me was evident—in their sighs, and tones of resignation— though they halfheartedly denied it, on the rare occasions we spoke about it. I noticed that my dad finally stopped making fun of my sister for wanting to be a teacher. I guess he thought that jokes about low salaries wouldn't land as well, when in his eyes, I had chosen to accept lesser prospects for myself, in the only way that really mattered. I wasn't going to be a dentist, nor a computer scientist, so what was I?

They thought they understood what I was going through. My mom had also been anxious when she started college, and my dad had been depressed when they had first divorced, so they knew that all I had to do was keep trying, and I'd just get over it like they had. They would just keep asking if I'd figured out what I was going to do yet, hinting with their tone that they were more than ready for me to get on with it, and tepidly claiming otherwise with their words.

I searched desperately for anything that I could manage to do. There was nothing that I *wanted* to do, except somehow survive on my own, so I didn't have to feel my parents' shame. I tried refurbishing and selling technology; almost immediately, I got an angry email complaining about something they thought I had missed. I wasn't sure if it was really my fault or not, but that didn't stop me from feeling so stupid and ashamed that I gave up. I tried submitting web design proposals on a freelance work site; the first guy I submitted to wanted to have a video call to work out a few fine details, and I panicked and closed my account.

I even applied for a pizza delivery job, trying to fool myself into believing that it would be manageable, since I'd be driving more than talking to anyone. That wasn't true in the first place, because I'd have just as many or more chances to embarrass myself, not to mention that driving was nearly as bad, especially in unfamiliar areas. I at least managed to make it to the interview, where I then learned that drivers were sometimes also expected to sit in the store, and answer the phone. That's among the worst things possible for my anxiety, as I'm denied the ability to read people's expressions and mannerisms. To make matters more humiliating, someone I knew from high school was working in the store during my interview, and seemed to think it was hilarious that I had ended up there. The manager called me later to offer the position. I couldn't even answer the phone; I finally managed to call back later and decline.

I felt so pathetic and worthless. I literally couldn't do anything. I knew by now that my anxiety, so completely pervasive, could not possibly always be logical; even if it was sometimes, I recognized specific instances when I was worrying about things that were extremely unlikely to happen, or assuming that someone *would* dislike me soon, before even I saw the smallest sign that they *did*. And yet, I could seemingly do nothing to stop myself from fleeing in shame. *Why can't I just grow the fuck up? It must be my fault. I'm just not trying hard enough. Anxiety is just an excuse.* These thoughts went through my head constantly.

I knew they must be true, because I couldn't even finish a project all on my own. Writing books, writing music, developing small video games—these weren't easy or reliable sources of income, but they could have been something. I should have known how to do these things, yet I could rarely bring myself to try, and never got anywhere before giving up. What possibility was there, other than that I was a lazy piece of shit?

I helped around the house, cooked meals sometimes, and helped with my dad's projects when he asked, but I knew it wasn't enough. Some days, I couldn't even find the energy to do those things, and I felt extremely guilty. My parents and sister offered well-meaning suggestions, but never understood or remembered my explanations as to why I couldn't manage *that* easy job, either, and became extremely frustrated with me. They said they were only trying to help because they cared about me, but it felt more to me like they were desperately searching for a way to rid their houses, and minds, of my depressing burden.

My brother graduated high school, two years after I had. My sister graduated college, and started working as a teacher. I was twenty years old, and still completely useless. I thought about suicide multiple times every day. I hated being alive, and I wasn't doing anyone else any good. I still feared failure too much to try to end my life, but I didn't know how much longer that would last. The effects of constant social anxiety and depression had combined to create a passive anxiety—a persistent sensation of dread over nothing in particular; a constant sickness in my stomach, and pain in my chest. I resolved to see a psychologist, finally deciding that it couldn't make me feel any worse than I did now.

I endured the dread leading up to the intake appointment, in no small part because I knew my brother would be driving me. Over the course of that appointment, I met the doctor I had settled on seeing. He seemed nice enough; not a whole lot like me, but maybe that wasn't surprising of someone with a medical degree. I told him that my main issue was depression; I thought it was probably caused by my anxiety, but maybe if I could just make myself care about life more, I could get over the anxiety. I shared that I had frequent suicidal thoughts, but also told him I knew I wouldn't attempt anything, which was only mostly true.

He explained that he would be using cognitive behavioral therapy (CBT) to try to help me. This essentially meant that he'd be trying to explain to me the ways in which my thoughts and beliefs, about myself, and what others thought about me, might be unhelpful and illogical, while simultaneously developing coping strategies to help me correct the behaviors—caused by these distorted feelings—that gave me trouble. That sounded unconvincing. Admittedly, I had come into therapy without any hope of success, as is often the case for depressed people.

But the strategy itself didn't seem helpful for me: I already had the insight into myself that CBT was supposed to provide. At least in some moments, I knew that I had lower self-esteem than I should have; I knew that others weren't judging me as constantly and harshly as it felt like they were; I knew that, when most people felt bad because of what someone else said, they reminded themselves that the other person didn't know them as well as they knew themselves, and let it go, and continued about their lives; I knew that just because someone that should have been close to me, like a family member, treated me like I had done something wrong, that didn't always mean I had.

But my self-esteem really was that low, even though that meant I wasn't seeing the whole picture; I really didn't enjoy any of the small things I knew I already had before; I really did feel, at the smallest sign, that everyone I spoke to disliked being around me; it did feel like a deeply personal admonition to receive mild criticism; and I really did wonder how anyone was supposed to like me, if my own family didn't seem able to. I just didn't get how to change these feelings.

I tried to explain this to him, but he seemed to just smile it off. Maybe he just thought I didn't realize *all* the different ways I was illogically hurting myself. Throughout our appointments, he continued to address the ways in which he viewed my thoughts and beliefs as being distorted. I usually agreed, explaining that I had already considered that. What I didn't understand was, how I was supposed to change these feelings? According to him, I was just supposed to choose to change them, now that I know they're based on assumptions, rather than on reality. Could religious people choose to forsake their faith, upon first learning that it's only a belief, not based on currently-tangible proof?

In my opinion, there's a point at which that becomes very difficult. Your experiences form your beliefs, which then determine what experiences you'll seek in the future. After years of reinforcement, this cycle is not easily escaped. You can't simply choose to change beliefs that have been constantly fortified by the events of your life. If you want to change them, then somehow, you must force yourself to experience those things that don't fit your beliefs, over and over again. For someone with immense anxiety and self-hatred, these experiences—genuinely positive interactions with others—seem hidden from our lives, impossible to trust in, and torturous to endure. We can feel helpless to even escape from the experiences we continue to have, which reinforce our current beliefs.

Each appointment made me feel worse than the last. I hadn't expected to make immediate progress, but I also hadn't expected to feel even more confused, more wrong about my own thoughts. My doctor wasn't rude, but he was very confident that his approach was correct for me, and seemed to disregard my explanations as to why I didn't believe it was helping. Each time I failed to act as if we'd made some breakthrough, he only seemed to become more confident that the problem wasn't that the technique was inapplicable to me, but rather that I was completely wrong about what my own thoughts and beliefs were, and that if I would just put in more effort, I would see that, and then they'd change.

Throughout the process, I was diagnosed with social anxiety disorder and major depressive disorder. Eventually, I think my doctor realized that I hadn't been exaggerating; I really understood how wrong I was, but I just didn't know how to get over it. CBT can be greatly beneficial for people who haven't yet considered themselves on a deeply personal level; people who need the helpful eyes of another to see the ways they're being unfair to themselves. I already knew I was being unfair to myself, but that was how I'd learned to manage the experiences I'd been through. In my opinion, CBT will not necessarily teach people how to be more fair to themselves, and that's what I believe most people with avoidant personality disorder need more than anything.

But nearly two more years would pass before I would hear of AvPD. My doctor apologized, but believed that he would be unable to help me, and suggested that we cease treatment. I agreed, and he recommended that I visit a psychiatrist instead. If his words wouldn't help me, perhaps another shot at pharmaceuticals would. I wasn't counting on it; I knew that a whole lot of people dealing with anxiety and depression never found a medication that helped, and not for lack of trying. But I'd still be trying something, and it would probably be a bit less stressful than therapy.

I had two months to wait until my first appointment. I started to have what I now know to be AvPD "fantasizing", or intrusive thoughts. I hadn't daydreamed before, but now trying to work on personal projects often resulted in my brain following a distracting, discomforting tangent. I would imagine myself as having completed something nice, and now I was discussing the merits of it with someone that was genuinely interested and impressed; then, the fantasy would end, and I would be crushed by the reality that the dream was unrealistic for anyone, especially me.

I had a nagging feeling that the diagnoses I had received did not tell my whole story, so I did some research on my own. I read about a couple diagnoses that felt familiar, yet not quite right. It seemed that I had many of the symptoms of inattentive ADD: I made careless mistakes; I was easily distracted from focus; I failed to complete tasks I worked on; I never kept anything organized; I procrastinated on doing things that required mental exertion; and I was quite forgetful, in both the short and long term. Perhaps this was my problem, and these issues were what had caused me to feel so bad about myself, and so anxious around others. Maybe treating these symptoms specifically would be helpful.

But thinking that made me feel like I was reaching; like it wasn't the root of my issues. I read about autism, and that seemed a little closer: difficulties in social interactions, misunderstanding social cues, restricted interests, and high sensitivity to sensory input, especially sounds; these were all things that I experienced, and people with autism often do. I had met a few autistic people, and I didn't particularly relate to them, but since autism is a spectrum disorder that can present itself in a variety of ways, it seemed like a possibility.

I arrived at my new doctor's office ten minutes before my appointment time, and checked in. I sat in the waiting room, more anxious by the minute as people came and went; over an hour later, the doctor was finally ready to see me. The appointment itself was brief. I told him about the issues I was having; he asked the usual sorts of questions about whether I had tried this for anxiety, or that for depression, before confidently informing me that we'd get it under control. He started me on a new prescription. He asked if I had any questions, and I asked for his opinion about the things I'd read, particularly whether I might have autism. He laughed, and said without further elaboration that he didn't think I was autistic, but that I could fill out a questionnaire about it before I left if I wanted, and he'd address it at the next appointment.

I did want to. The next appointment wasn't that far off, either; for some reason, I had to check in often, even when there was expected to have been no change, in order to keep my prescription. Again, I was early, and again, my appointment started much later than it was supposed to. The doctor asked if I'd been taking my medicine, and I told him I had; he asked if there were any changes, and there weren't; well, he said, we hadn't expected them this fast, so keep at it.

Within minutes, he was sending me out. I asked about the autism questionnaire. He just smiled and told me I didn't have autism. I now know that was true—the biggest giveaway being that, rather than having difficulty noticing social cues, I see them constantly, and read into them deeply—but the doctor dismissively passed on clarifying his reasoning to me.

These appointments felt like a huge waste of time, someone else's money, and what little mental energy I had, but I kept it up for a while. After ten weeks or so, my prescription was changed again, having done nothing. After ten weeks more of short, late appointments, and another new prescription still having done nothing, I was so tired of it. I quit taking the medicine and canceled my next appointment, saying I'd reschedule later. That was the last contact I had with the office.

The next year-and-a-half were the darkest days of my life. I knew my depression would never improve, because I didn't enjoy anything. I knew my anxiety would never improve, because I could hardly even manage to talk to my own family without my heart rate skyrocketing. Doctors, talk therapy, and medicine couldn't help me, because there was nothing strong enough to make me forget the shame I'd lived in for years.

My living situation continued to get more stressful, in ways that are very personal and painful to think about; but, in short, at the beginning of 2020, the foreclosure process began on my mom's house, where I was living. I was suffocated by guilt, feeling completely worthless as I was unable to help, but also trapped by the certainty that I literally couldn't force myself to just grow up and work like a normal person, no matter how terribly I felt. Neither of my parents, then or since, felt up to assuaging that guilt in me; they made it clear that, as much as they didn't want to make me feel bad, I *could* have done something if I cared.

I had moved out of my bedroom around the same time as that news came; our upstairs HVAC system had failed, and my mom insisted that we both sleep downstairs. I lost any personal space that I had, and with it, my privacy. I knew that, sometimes, I was just too anxious and depressed to handle a conversation with anyone, but now that I had no door to close, I could only hope that Mom would recognize when I just couldn't talk to her. Even with my repeated explanations of why this was, and that it was nothing personal, and that it was all my own fault, she didn't understand. She is the type of person that always seeks comfort in talking to others; each time I couldn't give that to her, she saw it as a sign that I hated her.

I didn't. I hated myself completely. I woke up and went to sleep with tears in my eyes and pain in my chest. Nothing I did brought happiness to myself, or anything of worth to anyone else. On one particularly horrible day, my mom particularly miserable and angry over the loss of her home, I checked to make sure I still knew where she kept her handgun, feeling that, when she'd leave briefly the next day, I'd finally be ready to use it on myself. I knew that everyone else would, eventually, be happier with me gone. I didn't feel like I cared anymore about what might happen to me if I messed up. But, I realized, I could still make things harder for everyone else if I messed up. For that reason, or maybe because I was just lying to myself about my own lack of fear, I never went back for the gun, settling instead to sob in complete hopelessness.

The COVID-19 lockdowns began. It was mildly amusing, in a melancholic way, to read about others' first experiences in isolation, while nothing changed for me. Well, one thing changed: our foreclosure was frozen. I spent months in the same state of constant panic, expecting that the pandemic was only delaying the inevitable. In the end, that wasn't the case: my mom kept her house. I felt, on one hand, a great relief, and on the other, the certainty that nothing had changed for me; every aspect of my self-hatred, especially the guilt, lingered on.

But, a couple months later, I first read the three words that might have begun, ever so slowly, to change everything: *avoidant personality disorder*. I don't remember where I first read them, because on that day, I read and watched every article and video I could find about AvPD, endlessly emotional in the certainty that I had, at long last, learned what it was called to be the way I was. There were other people exactly like me, facing the same fears of others' thoughts about them, and shame over their own existence. There was so little information available, but it was so much more than I'd had.

Knowing it might not have changed anything about what I could do, but it immediately began to change how I felt about myself. My anxiety and self-hatred were not imagined, nor had they come from nowhere: I had learned them from patterns in my life experiences. I had been continually reassured in my flaws, and rarely in my strengths. No one specific instance of horrible abuse or trauma had to exist to warrant the way I felt. Every little moment added up, and the encouragement that wasn't there meant every bit as much as the discouragement that was. Turning points in my life were less about new, big things that happened, and more about subtle changes, which caused me to recontextualize my previous experiences. The ways that this had changed my behavior came across as illogical in the context of some experiences, but it made perfect sense as a strategy for protecting myself from the pain I had known so many times.

I immediately began looking for a doctor that knew anything about avoidant personality disorder. I wanted to get an official diagnosis—not for myself, but for my family. I had to believe that, then, they would understand me. I didn't want to blame anyone for the past; I just wanted them to know for the future. I wanted them all to know, and to know why, that it really was terrifying, exhausting, to talk to a single stranger for a matter of minutes, even while family or friends were with me, and that the mistakes I felt I made would do more than just ruin that one day. I wanted them to know that the social anxiety they had experienced in certain situations, the depression they had experienced at certain times, while completely valid, just wasn't quite the same as what I was dealing with.

I wanted my brother to know that, sometimes, I just couldn't manage the random banter, and find everything funny, and just act casual. It didn't mean he was doing anything wrong, but sometimes, maybe more often than he'd think, I just needed some quiet. I wanted my sister to know that I appreciated her suggestions, but that the things that seemed easy to her weren't easy for everyone; that there wasn't necessarily a medicine guaranteed to work for each of us.

I wanted both of my parents to know that, when I forgot about something they'd asked me to do, or couldn't remember how to help them with something they thought was simple, it wasn't because I was ignoring them, or because I didn't care. I wanted them to know that every criticism or roll of the eyes nowadays hurt me deeply, but also that all those which had come from them before had made it hard for me to trust them, and that I hoped they could be patient if I was reluctant to confide in them.

I wanted Dad to know that I wasn't just lazy; I wasn't enjoying the "free time" I had by not working or learning, and I felt constant, extreme guilt that I couldn't provide for myself. I wanted Mom to know that what I had been through, even if it didn't seem like much, made it painful for me to express most emotions; made it sickening for me to make any physical contact with another, much less to give a hug; and that just because I often needed to be distant, that didn't mean I hated her. I wanted to ask for their patience, kindness, and respect, so that I could try to offer them the same.

It took a long time to find a doctor that seemed like a good candidate, and longer, due to the pandemic, to get an in-person appointment. When I finally did, in the summer of 2021, I knew immediately that the doctor I had chosen would not be a good long-term fit for me; his tangible lack of confidence in my understanding of myself, and his evident belief that he understood my problems better than I did, made me feel much worse about myself over the span of such a short appointment. That was OK—all I wanted, for now, was to get through the psychiatric evaluation.

The evaluation itself was a little while later. It was administered by a different doctor, and took a few hours. It included a whole bunch of things, including a few intelligence tests, intended to ensure that a learning disability wasn't possibly contributing to the patient's struggles—full-scale IQ, pattern recognition, explanations of abstract concepts. I smiled inside during the vocabulary section; the last word I was asked to spell was "pusillanimous", and having randomly looked up synonyms for the word "cowardly", while designing items for a video game I knew I'd never finish making, had paid off in this insignificant way. Then came the actual mental health bits, including a massive "how much do you agree with this statement?" multiple choice test, and an interview, in which the doctor asked similar sorts of questions, which I would answer in my own words, and expose my mannerisms in doing so.

More than a month later, I received my test results, in the form of a written report. It was quite long, starting with an incomprehensive record of the things I'd said. The doctor offered occasional analysis, such as that I'd "appeared disheveled" during the process, which I tried not to read too much into. I hadn't had any standout issues on the intelligence tests. Finally came the scores and analysis related to mental health and personality traits.

I was diagnosed with persistent depressive disorder —and avoidant personality disorder. I had known it was coming, and I was still overcome by emotion: a strange mix of resignation and relief, that I really had a name for my life experiences. The doctor mentioned that I also had significant levels of traits associated with paranoid personality disorder and dependent personality disorder, but neither to the extent that a diagnosis was applicable. The report concluded by offering me treatment advice—things like getting plenty of sleep, exercising, eating well, trying to jump back into the workforce, and attending both individual and group therapy. I can't say I was hearing any of it for the first time.

I went home with the report, ensuring the doctor that I'd reach out if I decided I wanted to continue into therapy with him. My brother had driven me again, and was the first to know about my diagnosis. I had already told him I knew I had AvPD, and I think he had already believed me, so he wasn't surprised. We went back to my dad's house, where my brother was living at the time; my dad was at work. I planned to sit there nervously for a time, considering how I would broach the topic with my mom, especially. I knew she would want to see the report, and I didn't want to let her—I didn't want to let her see how she'd made me feel, how that'd contributed to the insecurities I had, and how my doctors had heard what I'd had to say, and agreed. All I wanted was for her to understand who I was now.

Suddenly, my dad drove up, on one of the rare occasions he actually took his lunch break, rather than just working through the day. Suddenly, I was talking to him about my personality disorder. He looked through the report, and immediately fixated on what I'd feared he would: the IQ tests.

What stood out to him the most wasn't that I'd just been diagnosed with a personality disorder, or what I'd felt I had to say about the ways he'd acted towards me. What stood out was how smart I was, in a meaningless academic sense, based on a three-digit integer from a semi-randomly-generated test. What stood out was that I needed to figure out how to use that potential; not to be able to comfortably interact with other human beings, not to be able to love myself, but to build a career—to "succeed", as I'd always known he was dying for me to. He didn't say all of this in a rude way: just matter-of-factly. I had realized that this was probably how he would react as soon as the doctor handed me the report, saying the same sort of thing: *yes, you were right, you have a personality disorder, but I think you're smart, so no big deal!*

My sister and mom both had mild, sympathetic reactions. I was feeling discouraged, as usual, so when no one asked many questions, I just let it go. I slowly learned the truth: even people that really cared about me didn't necessarily have the emotional bandwidth to care about my mental disorder. Many times in the intervening months, I would explain to someone an aspect of my issues, and how the way I acted didn't mean I didn't care or wasn't trying, and how I might need just a little more help or consideration than someone else. They rarely understood, and almost never remembered later. I had to come to accept that, while that didn't mean they didn't care, it might mean that I can't afford to give so much of myself to them; to them, so much of my effort appeared as so little.

I wanted to share my own story, to help others that couldn't find any information about AvPD, or even the realization that it was a real thing that existed. I tried, but it took a long time to find the courage: to believe that I had anything useful to say; to convince myself that I wasn't just vying for attention; to just speak to others, when I was still so anxious, and depressed, and going nowhere with myself. But around the time of my twenty-fourth birthday—four months ago at the time I'm writing this—a very odd feeling hit me, and hasn't left.

It's a mix of desperation, and hope. It coalesced from many different thoughts I had. I thought about the age bands usually used on surveys, and realized that I'm about to leave the "18-24" group, the "college-age" group. I thought back to school, and realized that, in spite of the social anxiety, I had sometimes gotten real enjoyment out of being around others; it had just been easier to believe I hadn't, because it was so difficult to make it happen. I thought about all the things that I needed to be able to do, that I wanted to be able to do, for myself and for others, that I hadn't figured out. I thought about how I needed to be realistic about the person I was, and the person I could be. I thought about how it was my choice to decide who the people I have around me are, and how I should consider what they brought to my life as well as what I brought to theirs.

And, though it took a long time and made me very uncomfortable, I thought about love. I realized that I didn't have to let my parents' failed marriage, and their feelings towards me—well-meaning, but often in contradiction of their actions towards me—be the best thing that love ever could be for my own life. Love, for me, would be finding someone that appreciates what I am, enough to help me overcome what I am not, and myself doing the same for them. I realized that I wanted to find that, perhaps more than anything else, and that perhaps someday I could, because I'm not without worth.

My general, passive anxiety had been ramping up tremendously. My intrusive AvPD daydreams were becoming more frequent; now, they weren't just fantasies of successes with personal projects, triggered by working on those projects. Now, they were also about relationships with others: sometimes, imagined friendships, and often imagined romantic relationships; near-constant dialogues in my head that taunted me with things that could be, but weren't, not for me.

I also began to have fantasies about my own death—I had experienced those before, but now they were becoming much more frequent. It wasn't the same as having suicidal thoughts—these thoughts were more intrusive, and more specific; more related to the lack of the feeling I wanted so badly, that someone really cared that I was still here, rather than about currently wanting to die. I still feel *that* feeling often, as well, but just a bit less. The way I'm feeling now sort of feels like my last chance, but it's also my best chance—I know what I need; I know that I'm going to feel just as bad, now, not trying to get it, as I will if I do finally try. My anxiety, my depression—they're still hurting me as much as ever, but now I'm going to fight them, in the ways that are right for me.

Now all that was left was the hardest part: moving forward. Eleven days after my birthday, I recorded and uploaded my first video about AvPD to YouTube. I was sick with anxiety, thinking that I said nothing useful, that I left all the important bits out, that I sounded like a robot, and misspoke constantly, and cussed like a sailor, but I promised myself I wouldn't delete it. Soon, I began receiving comments, as others shared their own, similar experiences, or let me know that I had helped them feel a bit less alone, or thanked me for my bravery. I continued posting videos over the months. So many people have said so many nice things to me, which I still don't quite believe I deserve to hear, but that I appreciate so much more than I could ever tell them. It still makes me feel terribly anxious to post anything, but if I hear that it's helped one person, it makes me feel so much better.

It's helped me so much, personally. I finally got the strength to try what I knew I would never succeed at— writing a book about my experiences with AvPD. I had given up so many times trying to just write a fun, fictional story; how would I manage to write this? It was painfully difficult—but I did it. I cried a few times: writing about tearing out my hair and chewing holes into my fingernails; feeling worthless when I couldn't manage marching band or a simple job; specific times when I was certain I was ready to die; now, feeling the effects of impostor syndrome, thinking about how so many people have gone through so much worse, and turned out so much better.

But the hardest thing about creating this book was writing about my parents. How can I be fair to them—not just the people I know them as, but the people they were in their childhoods, before their own experiences changed them? How can I do that, and still be fair to myself? I know they care about me. I don't want to hurt their feelings. But they also hurt me very deeply, for many years—with their decisions, their gestures, their words, and their silence. In many ways, they continue to do this now, even as I ask so earnestly for them to try—try to care not just about me as a son, but as the individual I am—so that I can try to trust them again.

I had to share many things that they did, things which I never wanted to share, because they're part of my own story—they're why I am who I am. I couldn't mention every single thing they did that was alright, because while I am appreciative of those things, they weren't enough to change what ended up being my reality. I left some bad things out, too, because I don't have to mention every negative way they've ever made me feel to tell my story. I can only hope I chose the right things to say—to be forgiving, but to get the message across. Just admitting the truth makes me feel so guilty that I want, so badly, to publish this book under a name other than my own—but I have to learn to separate deep, crucial guilt from that which my disorder, and the sorts of experiences that caused it, impose upon me undeservedly.

I worry, too, about the possible reactions of anyone reading this book: that no one will understand how I feel, or how the experiences I recounted could have made me feel that way, or how my analysis of my own experiences makes any sense. I worry that people will think I'm whiny; will feel like I'm blaming others, and not taking enough responsibility for myself. Maybe you'll think I'm just cringey or unlikeable. But I also know that I told my own truths, and that I'm going to keep pushing to make a life, for myself, that I can be happy with—and I know that that has to be good enough for me. And I do believe that at least one person will feel at least a bit less alone after reading this, and that's all I really want from it.

GETTING TO KNOW US

I just talked about myself enough for a lifetime. Let's add you to the equation! In saying that, I'm assuming (for this chapter, and the next) that you're a person who doesn't have avoidant personality disorder. I want to tell you why, without knowing you personally, I think you might like to get to know someone with AvPD, whether you know they have it or not. I want to give you some idea of how they might seem different, and why; how (and why) you can be comfortable with their differences; and how to demonstrate that comfort to them, so that they might feel a similar comfort with you.

I want to do all of this while keeping *you* in mind. People with AvPD are very conscious of how much time, energy, and emotion is invested to engage with another person, and only feel comfortable if a friendship is at least as beneficial for you as it is for us. At the end of the day, some people just don't mesh very well with us extra-anxious people, and we get that!

I'll go through a few ascending "tiers" of relationships. Maybe you'd like to just feel a little less caught off-guard next time you have a one-off conversation with an awkward stranger. Perhaps you have an anxious classmate or coworker you have to interact with regularly, and you wish it was just a bit less weird. Possibly, you have a close friend, relative, or partner that still seems a bit uncomfortable or distant with you. I'd like to share some insights from my own experiences that might help you feel a bit better in these situations.

Hopefully, many of them will be helpful in a variety of awkward situations; only a handful are super-specific to people with AvPD. Some of the "higher-tier" advice can also apply to more casual scenarios, if someone seems like they might be awesome enough that it's worth the extra effort to get through to them. Even if some or all of this seems inapplicable to you, or you're the socially anxious one in the equation, I think you'll find some of it worth thinking about. Lastly, I want to mention that for these scenarios, we'll assume that the anxious person in question is just anxious, and not actively rude—and is also making efforts at improving themselves (which is the subject of the final chapter).

STRANGER SMALL-TALK

For the first tier, I decided to think from the perspective of a stranger I might have spoken to during my brief enrollment at college—outside of classes, just walking around campus. Even avoiding social interaction as much as I possibly could, I met a few people who could have been new friends. These are people that had no particular reason they *had* to talk to me, and weren't necessarily expecting any long-term benefit for having done so; they were just making conversation, passing time, maybe growing their social group, as people that are naturally extroverted (or trying to pass as such) often do.

To me, this represents a "natural" interaction between two people, with as few additional variables as possible. Either one of us can bail on the interaction at any time, for any reason, after which there's a good chance we'll never even see each other again. If this theoretical acquaintance and I can't get at least a bit comfortable around each other in short order, that's exactly what will happen. Maybe it will anyway, but might as well be more comfortable while we're passing the time, right?

Let's pretend that you're this other person, and I'm a random guy you meet who, unbeknownst to you, has AvPD. I never start a conversation I don't have to—I assume you're probably not interested in talking to me, and I don't want to waste your time or make you uncomfortable—so it's you that decides to start a conversation. That brings us to the first thing you might want to know about people with AvPD: it's not a matter of whether or not we're currently anxious, but how anxious we currently are. There are many layers to the anxiety we experience, one of which is what I call passive social anxiety. When any other person can perceive my existence by any means, I am constantly worried that they are thinking something negative about me, before I have any reason at all to believe that.

In our scenario, that means I might come into the conversation with the expectation that I've unknowingly done something to inconvenience or discomfort you. You might notice signs of unease in my demeanor. When you speak to me, I might respond as quickly as possible, minimizing the number of syllables leaving my mouth, and maximizing the speed at which I blurt them out. You might become a bit unsettled yourself, wondering if I'd rather you ended the conversation. Truthfully, I'm probably a bit conflicted. Impromptu conversations make me very anxious, but I know they can be awesome: I've made good friends, my only friends, by chatting with the people that chose to approach me randomly. I'm a normal guy—I have a sense of humor, interests I'd like to share, things I'd like to do with other people—and I'd like to build a variety of new relationships.

So how can you make these awkward conversations more comfortable for yourself, and how can you tell if another person is disinterested in talking to you, or just anxious? There are some mannerisms you can demonstrate which help me—and by extension, you—feel, and act, more at ease. These mannerisms can also help lead the conversation to a natural resolution—whether that is you politely ending the encounter, or myself becoming more comfortable, and opening up a bit. Though I never expect these sorts of gestures, I always appreciate them, and I think they're simple and valuable tools for helping you enjoy interactions with a variety of people.

Something simple, and potentially quite helpful, that you probably already practice sometimes is what I'll call *emotional normalization*. Have you ever spoken to someone, so naturally happy and outgoing, that they reacted a bit more positively than seemed warranted, to anything you said? When you encounter someone like this, you likely "normalize" their emotions in your mind. You assume they truly feel happy or excited, but maybe not as much as you would have to, to show as much emotion as they are. Maybe you're that super-positive person, and you've learned to assume that people feel better inside than they seem, to you, to show through their reactions.

This second one is usually a helpful assumption to make about socially anxious people! I want to express positive emotions, but it's unbelievably difficult for me to do so. If you tell me about something interesting that you do, I'll probably nod, say "ah, cool," in a near-monotone, and try my best to make eye contact for a fraction of a second. Most people see this as an underreaction, and a rude hint that I'm not interested in talking to them. Please don't take it that way! If you can see by my mannerisms that I'm probably anxious, not annoyed, then normalize my emotions. How would you have felt if I said "Oh, that's really cool!", while smiling and making eye contact? That's what I wish I had done, and how I wanted to make you feel.

An important element of building comfort with anyone is to learn something about them. With highly extroverted people, that might require no effort on your part; with others, you might have to ask some simple questions. Some sorts of questions are easier to offer satisfying answers to, especially when you're asking someone with social anxiety. If you ask me a "closed" question (yes or no?), I will probably answer with a single word, because I don't want to waste your time saying things I'm not sure you care about hearing. If you ask me an "open" question (what's the most interesting thing you've ever done?), I will probably freeze up, not having an easy answer ready; and, not wanting to anxiously ramble like a moron, I will shrug and say "I don't know, I'm kinda boring."

If you get either of these sorts of non-responses from someone that seems anxious, again, don't immediately assume it means they don't want to talk to you. Try widening or narrowing the scope of your question; add a little information about yourself each time, so it doesn't feel like an interrogation. Maybe give one topic a couple tries, and then move on to another. I'm not guaranteeing there's a question that will get you a response right now. There's always the possibility that someone is just not in the mindset to talk, but once you've struck up a conversation, it's worth giving it a good shot.

There's a good chance you'll want to ask them about the things they're interested in. People with AvPD in particular would probably love to talk about their interests, rarely getting chances to do so, but will be reluctant to for fear of judgment. Before you ask, try to get them on the same page. Volunteer some information about your own interests, not just listing them off, nor lingering on one for forever—the same moderation you'd use in any conversation. If they're into any of the same things, they might speak up on their own. If not, ask them in a general way that doesn't require them to take explicit stances on your interests, and ideally leaves them a relatable "out".

If you mention that you play basketball in the public park once a week, don't ask if they shoot hoops—

instead, follow up by asking if they get to do much of anything outside, what with how hot it is. If they do play basketball or another sport, that will be the first thing they think to mention; if they grow a garden, they might feel comfortable enough to mention that; if they never leave their house, they might not feel like you'll judge them harshly over that, since you know how damn hot it is outside. If you can manage a little self-deprecation, then casually tease yourself about your interests—for the basketball example, if you're not super tall, a joke about your height might come to mind. As long as you don't overdo it, that can be a great icebreaker for anyone, and especially for an anxious person, who can probably relate, and might feel reassured that you won't feel the need to make fun of them, instead.

If you really want to go the extra mile to help an anxious stranger act more comfortably around you, you can try what I'll call the *State of Selective Obliviousness*, or *so-so*. Like with any conversation, you're listening to what I'm *trying* to say, with my words, hand gestures, or anything else, and reacting in a way that's relatable. The key to *so-so* is that you can also recognize what I'm unconsciously saying—or not *trying* to say—and deliberately ignore these things, letting them have no effect on your reaction. When I barely glance in your direction, make an uncomfortable face, and shuffle around awkwardly, remember that you didn't do anything wrong—that's just my uncertainty showing. When I speak in a shaky voice, I *am* saying that I'm anxious around you, but I'm not *trying* to—it was supposed to be a secret, until my body betrayed me.

I'd prefer you didn't tell me that it's alright to be anxious, because that only reinforces how I feel—that people can instantly feel my discomfort. Speak on undeterred, as if you didn't even notice, even if I'm certain you must have. Yes, I'm still anxious; you aren't going to convince me that you really don't notice. But you can show me that it makes so little difference to your comfort that you don't even react; that we're having an interesting conversation, which has very little to do with me and my anxiety.

It's hypocritical for me to ask that of you—even when all logic suggests that I am safe, my anxious instincts insist otherwise. Who am I to tell you not to let my awkwardness make you uneasy? But there's a very good chance you have more self-confidence than I do. If you can, now is the time to try to use it, and share it with me. If you're very good at *so-so*, or you just naturally pay no mind to people's anxious mannerisms, being just a little bit bubbly or over-the-top (in positive attitude, not volume of voice) can help me stop focusing on how anxious I am about myself, and become drawn in to your personality. Keep the setting in mind—the more people are around, the more I prefer a subdued atmosphere. The possibility of other people noticing us and joining the conversation is overwhelming to me.

In short, if you give us easy things to talk about, and show us you don't care that we're acting a little weird, then you're honestly making us more comfortable than most of the people we've spoken to throughout our lives. Anything else is icing on the cake.

ANXIOUS ACQUAINTANCES

The next tier of interaction is with anxious acquaintances—friends-of-friends, classmates, coworkers, or anyone else who seems alright, and is around a lot, but wouldn't necessarily be considered a friend. Almost all of what I want to say about these sorts of interactions with socially anxious people is about your own expectations and understanding, and not anything you need to do or say—just so you can be more comfortable around people you end up seeing often, anyway. If it does happen that you are working or learning with someone that has AvPD or similar traits, they will likely notice and appreciate any comfort you have around them, and even if they are unable to reflect it, they may be inclined to be as kind and helpful to you as they can.

As you might have gathered from my thoughts on the concept of emotional normalization, socially anxious people in particular often have a strong dissonance between how they feel inside, and what they express outwardly. Among the things people often begin to expect of their acquaintances, to some degree, is empathy. You might groan to them about having been up all night studying, or vent about how your boss is a pain in the ass, or just grumble about life in general. You aren't expecting them to offer their deepest sympathies or come up with solutions—just to show some surface-level solidarity.

With a socially anxious person, you might find that they just don't do this. When I have had to externally empathize with an acquaintance, I would usually end up just nodding, pursing my lips, and saying "yeah..." in a mildly-exasperated, low tone of voice. People tended to assume that, either I somehow had no capacity to relate to the ubiquitous irritation they're complaining about, or seemingly more likely, I just disliked them personally.

I think it would make those people feel better to know that I didn't dislike them, and that I do actually empathize quite strongly—but only inside. You should expect that, if you're getting to know someone with severe social anxiety, they will probably not be able to show you much empathy, but that they will think it, and feel it more deeply than you can see. They will wish that they could show it to you, and they might try sometimes—but there's a good chance, especially if they have AvPD or similar traits, that any external empathy will appear negatively self-centered.

For example, when someone might normally say "yeah, all-nighters are hell, but at least the test will be out of the way after today", it might instead occur to me to chuckle, and mumble something about how I didn't bother to study, because I have no idea what's going on anyway—sometimes even if that wouldn't have been true (it usually would have been). I realize as soon as I say this that, rather than giving the person the validation and assurance they want, I've "upstaged" their complaint and made it awkward for everyone. I'm trying so hard to offer relatability, but it's infinitely easier for me to say unduly negative things about myself, and present matching emotions, than it is to regard the problem as an external force, and to share encouragement against it. Being positive is hard, especially for someone that constantly worries that someone will point out why any confidence in themselves is misguided. In short—we do empathize with your struggles, so try not to let our lack of effectively saying so get you down.

In the same vein, perhaps more specifically for people with AvPD than just general social anxiety, are our responses to compliments or congratulations. You could say the nicest thing anyone's ever said to me, and I might just mutter my thanks through a clearly-forced, lips-only smile. I'm not used to expressing positive emotions, and I'm similarly unfamiliar with receiving them. Trust issues and non-existent self-esteem mean that I have a bit of difficulty with believing that anyone who praises me actually means what they're saying, and far more difficulty believing that it's actually true about me, regardless.

This does not mean that I don't appreciate what you said. I can guarantee that, at a minimum, you made my entire day much better, and I'll never forget it. Unfortunately, I will have a very hard time communicating these feelings to you, and will just walk away, wishing I'd said more. The takeaway is that people with social anxiety appreciate earnest, believable praise as much as, or more than, anyone else would, but yet again might not be able to tell you—take my word that they do appreciate your kindness, and will try to gradually get that across to you.

One additional small-talk strategy I'd like to mention at this point is what I'll call *destination dialogue*. That's a fancy way of saying that we should have a conversation that seems to be progressing towards an end goal. You can start a conversation like that about any subject, and with only a few seconds of thinking ahead. Take any random small-talk opener, add any interest of yours to the mix, and find a simple path between the two. "The weather" is something that people stereotypically talk about just to break silence, but if you enjoy literally anything about being outside, there's an easy path from today's weather to sports, nature, urban exploration, or whatever else. That leads to a natural, complete conversation that can be politely dropped if they're not showing interest, or easily continued if they are.

There are actually many reasons why this can make me (and you) more comfortable. It's immediately clear that you're driving the conversation—I'm too anxious to say much past the basic response required by what you said. It's great if I feel confident that you can carry the conversation on your own, when I am not able to say much. I like to plan what I'm going to say to people ahead of time, so I don't say something stupid—if it feels like you started a conversation with an idea in mind, I can relate to you more. And since I'm so anxious, I'm always searching for a way out of any conversation, even if it seems alright for now. If I can see that you're bringing the conversation towards a natural conclusion, I can stop worrying about finding my own escape route, trusting that you'll leave one open for me. As a result, I'll be able to concentrate more intently on what you're saying, and I might actually be able to enjoy hearing it. This benefit also applies to you—you don't have to wonder if someone really doesn't want to talk to you, because you'll allow them a clear opportunity to decide if they'd like to drop it, or keep the conversation going.

Paradoxically, you might witness someone actually becoming more anxious with you, if you reach a certain level of comfort with them, without having really become friends. This is something I have experienced, and I imagine others with AvPD can relate to. If I am your distant acquaintance, I will assume that you are polite to me simply because you feel like you have to be; you are indifferent to me, at best, and more likely are uncomfortable around me. I'm not a fan of feeling like these assumptions are true, but I am used to it, and feel like little that I can do would change your opinion of me in either direction.

If, after a while, it strikes me that you seem to actually like being around me to some extent, I might have the anxious realization that your opinion of me now has room to be lowered; that any of the little, stupid things I do might make you suddenly dislike me. Of course, in practice, this will only make me act more weird around you. If an anxious person you are getting to know suddenly gets even worse about eye contact and awkward silences, don't read too much into it: don't change anything about how you're acting, and soon, they might be more comfortable than before.

FRETFUL FRIENDS

That takes us to the third tier of interaction: friendship! Yes, there probably exist socially anxious people that would like to be your friend. I never tried to make any friends, and I still ended up with a group of them that I talked to for years. At least one of them was among the least reserved and most extroverted people I've ever seen. I believe that people with avoidant personality disorder might actually be shockingly easy to befriend: if you have some commonalities in interests, sense of humor, or anything else, all that's left is to try to make us feel more comfortable than other people do. If what you've read in this chapter so far makes some sense (and even if half of it doesn't), then you've already got it in the bag.

The first thing I want to mention about becoming friends with someone dealing with social anxiety is almost the inverse of the paradox I previously mentioned. At some point, your anxious friend will realize that you care about them, on some personal level, and become much more comfortable with you. That might happen gradually, naturally, but for me, it tends to be a very sudden change, which is at least as jarring for me as it is for my new friend. I'll talk about subjects I might have been resistant to before, speaking and acting louder and more expressively. I'm doing that because I'm subconsciously excited about how comfortable I feel; it's probably an AvPD-specific thing, or maybe even me-specific.

But eventually, I'll probably do something that feels like "going too far"—maybe I'll react more excitedly to something than I usually do, and someone laughs at me —and in extreme embarrassment, I will revert to discomfort. Maybe I'll fall completely silent, unable to hold conversation for a while, or act panicky, or feel like I have to keep apologizing for whatever completely normal thing I did. If a new friend ever has this sort of reaction while getting comfortable with you, just be patient and keep acting the same way you have been. Soon, they'll find their comfortable normal.

Once you consider someone a friend, there's a good chance you'll think about hanging out with them outside of the setting you usually see them in. This can be difficult for someone with social anxiety. For one thing, we're assuming at this point that the person is not a "best" friend, and at least for some time is a "new" friend. They're nice to be around, but that doesn't mean you want to hang out with just them. The natural thing to do would be to invite them to hang out with some of your other friends. This might be less awkward for them, as well—but only if they already know (and generally like) these other friends, and only if there's not too many of them: maybe one or two others.

Many common hangout settings also present stressful situations for anxious people. Depending on the severity of the person's anxiety, this may just mean they'll avoid overtly social locations like bars; people-dense locations like movie theaters may also present an issue. Consider this when you're inviting them to do something: if you really want them to come, just remember that the less public the event, the better. If you already have something in particular you want to do, but you're not sure if they would want to come, it doesn't hurt to ask—just remember, if they decline, that it's likely due to their anxiety, and not because they don't want to hang out with you.

Particularly for people with AvPD or similar traits, the activities they are comfortable participating in might be limited, even in a private setting. Our fear of judgment and criticism is especially exacerbated around newer friends, as we don't want to mess it up. Particular areas of difficulty for me include things I haven't done before, things I feel like I'm not very good at, and things at which my friends have some expectation of how good I am, which I might disappoint. This encompasses many things, and as my new friend, you probably have no idea what most of these things are, much less that they will be problematic for me. It would be both impossible and uninteresting for you to plan your hangouts around this, so generally speaking, don't. If you really want to try, go for shared interests which involve as little aspect of performance or competition as possible.

Truthfully, all you need to do is keep their anxiety in mind. If they agree to come, but then mostly opt to stand around or watch, rather than actively participate, remember that it's probably because they're anxious, not bored or irritated. You can still include them by chatting with them; probably keep to a minimum the number of times you ask them about their participation. Sometimes they'll agree to come once, and then decline a similar invitation, and again, just remember that it's probably not anything you did wrong; they just misjudged their comfort.

Your best bet on getting an anxious person to accept an invitation is to be as specific as possible about what you're inviting them to—every person you're inviting, the exact location, any planned activities, an exact start time, and an approximate duration. There is a very good chance they will just say "no; thanks, though" the first time—whether because they're anxious about the event itself, or because, as is often the case for people with AvPD, they think you feel obligated to invite them. Leave a bit of time between invitations, but be persistent—eventually, when they are more confident you actually want them to come, they will likely either accept, or explain (in so many words) that the particular thing you invited them to sounds hard to handle.

One final thing to keep in mind about hanging out with anxious friends is that they will likely be very hesitant to invite anyone else to do anything. They might feel more comfortable inviting you and the rest of a group to hang out, after having accepted the invitations of others a few times. However, people with AvPD or similar traits might never extend invitations, even after accepting yours. This probably doesn't mean they were attending out of a feeling of obligation, or that they don't care enough to go to the effort to organize their own thing.

People like me tend to see two possibilities that could result from asking you to do something: the most likely, in our eyes, is that we'll be rejected. We'll feel bad for wasting your time, and stupid for asking, and have a hard time believing, regardless of any reason you give, that you weren't just uninterested. The other possibility is that you accept; then we'll have a hard time believing you didn't just do so out of a feeling of obligation, because it's hard to believe that anything we'd think of doing is interesting enough that you'd want to do it with us.

YOU, ME, AND AVPD

The final tier of relationships includes any with someone that you care about a lot, and expect, or hope, to have in your life for a long time—family members, best friends, or romantic partners. What I discuss in this section is not generally applicable to anyone dealing with social anxiety, and is more specific to my experiences with, and thoughts about, avoidant personality disorder. The previous sections included some things to think about, and some relatively simple conversational strategies, which might help you feel a bit better around anyone that seems less than comfortable.

This part is different. This is about understanding and accepting one person in particular that you really care about; helping them how you can, and knowing how you can't. It's also about how you can tell if they're trying their hardest to make it work, and how to keep in mind what's best for you. It will be theoretical for most readers, but it should still be engaging on an empathic level.

So, can you have a close relationship with someone with avoidant personality disorder, and would you ever really want to? Of course! If someone means that much to you, AvPD doesn't change what you already knew you liked about them. It should change some of your expectations about them. Some aspects of the disorder could make being around us feel painful or limiting to some people, but you might also appreciate things like how empathetic we tend to be (even if we're slow to show it outwardly), how cognizant we are of our current shortcomings, and the likelihood that we develop very strong attachments to those that care about us.

AvPD does not make someone unlovable, but like any other personality traits, these might be ones that you can handle in high doses, and they might not. In the end, AvPD is not a reason to care about someone, but if you care about them for other reasons, you'll have to care about their disorder, too. Most importantly, every person with AvPD still has to be considered as the individual they are. What follows are simply some things I would like to say to a person that wants to have a close relationship with someone that seems to have common traits of avoidant personality disorder.

If I could only tell that person one thing, it wouldn't be about any of the specific difficulties I face; it would be about what all of those various difficulties have common to their nature. AvPD is a personality disorder, and what that usually means is that it's here to stay. I can't change the things that caused it. There are some things I can try, generally with major limitations, to improve the symptoms. The most significant way I can improve myself is to try to limit my maladaptations. I have to try to live my life as if my anxiety (and resulting depression) isn't there, even though it is.

That means it's a never-ending struggle. That means that every single person with AvPD has to make their own decisions about the benefits and drawbacks of every single maladaptation they wish they could stop. That means that I'm constantly re-evaluating whether I'm currently doing the right thing for my mental health. That means that some days I'll seem to make huge progress, and some days I'll seem like I've lost it all.

Expect that if you're in a close relationship with someone with AvPD, they will be a bit sporadic—their emotions, their ability to focus, and their capacity to handle things out of their comfort zone. They kinda have to go with the flow, and if you're around them, you should, too. When they're up for trying things that they usually aren't, encourage them! Every time they succeed is progress—but that doesn't guarantee the same thing will be any easier next time. It might even be harder, for what seems like no reason to someone on the outside. It's really important to accept that, and manage your expectations—both for your own sanity, and so that you don't accidentally discourage them from trying, by making them feel like they got your expectations up, and then let them down.

Regardless of the exact nature of this relationship, you'll likely notice many ways in which the symptoms of the disorder manifest, including the maladaptations which individuals with AvPD have developed to protect themselves from some of the worst feelings that the symptoms cause. I want to share some advice on understanding and responding to these issues, with the goal of making both you and the person with AvPD happier. I'll go through them in four categories, starting with the one that might come up first and most frequently: public life.

If you've read everything up to this point, you're well aware of the fact that AvPD includes social anxiety, but it really can't be overstated how big of a deal it is for us. Someone that has managed their maladaptations well might have a quiet day job (perhaps part-time), a friend or two they hang out with in private or low-traffic public locations, and could make themselves go buy groceries if they absolutely had to, but probably gets them delivered. They will still most likely have constant fear of social interaction in public. When they are forced into those interactions, they are likely still hyper-analyzing themselves and whoever they're speaking to; feeling like they're making mistakes; seeing signs that others dislike them; having physical symptoms of discomfort such as pain and sweating; remembering how ashamed this makes them feel for a long time.

I would see this theoretical person as being on the high-functioning end of AvPD. Even this person, having managed their disorder much more successfully than I have until now, would likely be extremely uncomfortable with so many things that are just part of life for most people. Appointments with doctors, dentists, or mechanics are hell, from the minute you have to schedule them, to physically getting yourself to the location; waiting anxiously for someone to talk to you and wondering if you did something wrong; finally suffering through the appointment—it doesn't end until you're back home. If any appointments are not absolutely critical, you'll probably reschedule or cancel them instead. If your job sucks even more than most, you'll probably just live with it, rather than deal with the horrifying prospect of starting a new one; or, if things get bad enough, you'll just quit working. Things that many people consider fun outings—bars, restaurants, bowling alleys, arcades, concerts—tend to be torturous.

In a close relationship with someone dealing with this, the first thing you have to do is accept it. Most of us are extremely self-aware, and therefore realize that it's illogical to think that everyone notices our smallest missteps, and that their every move is a judgment against us, and that any criticism should make us feel ashamed of our entire existence. However, due to patterns we noticed in things we experienced while growing up, our brain enters panic mode anyway.

The human brain is not flawlessly logical, as you've probably experienced before, yourself, when choosing to procrastinate, or when making a compulsive decision. The brains of people with AvPD have learned to recognize more scenarios as being dangerous than a normal brain has, usually because our brains were trained on a biased dataset—for example, particular people repeatedly judging and criticizing us for the emotions we showed, and the things we liked, and the words we said; people we thought were smart, and trustworthy, and cared about us.

Sometimes, we will have a hard time managing the absolute minimum of public existence. It's not your responsibility to cover for us, but being patient with us goes a long way. If we think you understand that we're trying our best, that we're not just making excuses, and that we wish every bit as much as you do that we could *just do it*, we'll be more able to trust ourselves, and hopefully get back on top of it. Similar understanding can be applied to social outings that are supposed to be fun. If a family member refuses to go out to eat in a restaurant with you, that doesn't mean they don't love you. If your best friend declines a ticket you've already bought to their favorite band's concert, that doesn't mean they only hang out with you out of habit.

Understanding this reality doesn't mean you stop considering your own wants and needs, contextualized by the type of relationship you have with this person. If it's a good friend, maybe you can both be content to remain friends, while you also spend more time with other friends, more amenable to the activities you currently want to participate in. If it's someone you're dating, consider, like you would with any partner, how you might be willing to compromise, and how you aren't. Talk with them about it; be open to staying in the relationship if they are making you happy and putting forth effort, and be open to calling it quits if not. This area of the disorder is one of the most difficult to improve, and while they should continue to try (in ways I'll expound on later), being in a close relationship with them is most likely to work if you're happy just to be around them anyway. Depending on your personality and interests, it might feel boring, or even suffocating, to be around a person that hates being in public, or it might not matter much at all.

Other issues that often come with AvPD are likely more universally challenging, such as the many things that can be put under the umbrella of self-negativity.

When you spend a lot of time around someone with AvPD, you will likely notice a general depression, constant but fluctuating in severity, which comes in large part from their anxiety, the shame they feel, and the things they want to do, but are unable to, for themselves, and others, like you. This shows itself like it does in anyone else dealing with depression—low physical and mental energy; disinterest in most things, even which they might usually enjoy; inability to focus, even on simple conversations. Some of us have suicidal thoughts; some may keep them to themselves, while others may vocalize them in their hardest moments, before deeply regretting having done so later.

More specifically to people with AvPD is their low self-esteem: a lack of confidence in everything about themselves, which often extends to self-hatred. This again stems from biased experience patterns in their life, which taught them that they succeeded rarely, and messed up often, with their own goals, and in trying to be kind to others. It can manifest itself in different ways.

A person may seem quite comfortable around you in general, and suddenly become visibly anxious upon having to do something in front of you that requires any amount of knowledge, dexterity, or focus—even if it's something they do all the time. They may be reluctant to show you the results of anything they've worked on. They will likely be very modest in describing their aptitude at things they're actually quite good at, and give themselves little to no credit for anything else. Some, like I do, may use self-deprecation as a coping strategy to head off any chance of you criticizing, or sometimes just teasing, them about something they're insecure about, which is most everything.

They likely also experience a general anxiety of varying intensity—a feeling like desperation, which has no active cause, social or otherwise, and often includes physical discomfort such as stomach, chest, and head pain. In this generally anxious mood, I often get antsy—physically, mentally, emotionally, vocally—and I'm particularly sensitive to signs of judgment. For me, this anxiety intensifies when, at random, I can't help but dwell on inner conflict—between all the things I want to do, and the few things I'm able to manage. It almost seems to alternate with my surges in depression—I feel a bit better, I can think a bit clearer, and suddenly I'm dwelling intensely on the ways I wish I could improve, before I inevitably conclude that I'm doomed to never get where I want to be, and depression takes its turn again.

Someone you're close with feeling this negatively about themselves will probably bother you. You might feel bad for them, and then feel confused because you see them as a pretty good person with a pretty good life, and get irritated that they can't see the same. You might find it hard to stay in a good mood when they can't manage it. You might fear the possibility that they decide to hurt themselves. How can you handle this?

Give them space when they need it. Give yourself space when you need it. This is important for anyone, and particularly with people with AvPD. When you are with them, have a good time, however you do that with them. The more they realize that they are able to be happy, and that they are able to make you happy, the less important and validated their negative feelings about themselves will seem to them. You can also help build their confidence by offering positive reinforcement frequently, but casually—just quick, earnest bits of appreciation. If they have a tendency towards too much self-deprecation, you might try calling them out on it, in a somewhat opposite manner: rarely, rather than every time they do it, and taking the opportunity to explain, in personal terms, why they shouldn't do that to themselves so much.

You will likely also notice issues related to their ability to trust. Signs of this will likely be consistent, yet somewhat more subtle, because it's likely based on an unconscious, habitual inability to feel safe around others, rather than any amount of active distrust in you. It will probably affect their conversational habits more than anything else—they may be very uncomfortable talking about their interests, their work, or things that they are good at, out of fear of lowering your opinion of them, of raising your expectations of them. This is, again, because they've had many experiences before where these negative reactions were all they could expect. They will probably be hesitant to bring such topics up at all; if you ask about them, they might try to avoid saying much by turning the question on you as quickly as possible, or reaching for a segue to a different subject.

There may also be some reactionary, physical signs of trust difficulty, before any physical contact is involved. For example, I experience intense discomfort when people position themselves in particular ways relative to myself. The personal space I need to feel comfortable is significantly larger than most people's, being roughly equivalent to the six feet that you're probably now familiar with from social distancing guidelines.

However, I also have an aversion to having people nearby where I can't see them—direct line of sight is best, but being in the periphery of my vision is better than being behind me. I would also prefer to be where you can see me, so that I can feel that you're able to be comfortable, as well. I personally prefer that we are either facing each other, or that I am beside and slightly in front of you. I will move myself out of uncomfortable relative positions, if the situation allows it. If I can't move, you might notice me turning to glance at you sometimes, trying, and failing, not to appear as wary as I feel. If I am very comfortable with you, or extremely uncomfortable with where you are, I might ask you to move a bit.

This discomfort, for me, comes primarily from the element of surprise—not knowing what you're doing, or being able to read you, or feeling like you don't know what I'm doing. For others with AvPD, this may be rooted more in an actual fear for their physical safety. My assumption is that this would be more common in women with AvPD. That assumption is based on both unfortunate societal realities, as well as anecdotal evidence from some women with AvPD, who have shared their experiences with me through my YouTube channel. People that deal with this will likely have additional difficulties with this sort of trust that I am personally unfamiliar with.

Other trust difficulties are more personal and internalized, but you may occasionally see hints of them. A big one is guilt. The person with AvPD whom you are close with will probably feel indebted to you anytime you do anything nice for them, including emotionally. They will likely always feel like they are falling further behind, able to do less for you than you do for them, to some degree regardless of how true that might or might not be. These feelings develop from similar experience patterns as I've mentioned repeatedly, but may be exacerbated in young adulthood, particularly if they faced difficulties with self-sufficiency due to their social anxiety and depression. They likely dwell on this guilt frequently, but aren't likely to complain about it, since doing so would seem fruitless, and make another problem for you to have to think about. You may notice a tendency for them to thank you, for any help or kindness, primarily by apologizing profusely for inconveniencing you.

Relatedly, they may have a fear of the possibility of you abandoning them, which can have aspects of both dependency and paranoia. On one hand, they may feel that you do so much for them that they would be unable to survive without you (perhaps physically, but often socially or emotionally). On the other, their guilt causes them to feel that you are getting the short end of the stick; it would only make sense for you to abandon them, and they wouldn't blame you. Of course, if they care a lot about you, they don't want to believe this, and it can become an intense fear. Similarly to their social paranoias, they may see small things you do as signs that you're considering the possibility of leaving them behind.

All of these fears are general, but over time, they may develop some specific to you. They might find it hard to forget certain ways you may have made them feel when they were having a bad moment. These memories aren't grudges—the person doesn't care about you any less, and they likely blame their own hypersensitivity for how they feel.

Such feelings can, however, increase the person's uncertainties in themselves, and in whether they deserve their relationship with you. All that really needs to happen with these thoughts is that they be talked through, so that both parties can know that there are no hard feelings—or that, if there are, they can be handled. The person with AvPD may be slow to bring up these thoughts, as they do not want to make you feel guilty, but if the two of you speak honestly and openly often, in general terms, they will eventually mention if they have a hangup.

These aspects of AvPD are part of what can make the person you care about feel so distant from you. The good news is that they are likely quite malleable in this respect! Something like wide-ranging social anxiety is really hard to heal, since it involves constantly new experiences and sensory oversaturation. Trust issues can work their way out, on a personal level with you, after which the person may trust you more than they have ever trusted anyone. You'll likely want to handle each of the distinct issues in slightly different ways, though the key concepts can be boiled down to communication, respect, and patience.

If they seem to feel guilty about the nice things you do for them, or the kind ways you treat them, casually reassure them that you act the way you do because you care about them. Just leave it as an obvious implication that they don't need to feel indebted to you, except perhaps on occasions where they explicitly bring up that concern. With things like sharing interests, they will warm up the longer they maintain a high level of comfort with you. Just act naturally—you don't need to disguise disinterest, or fake interest that you don't have. Give them the same attention you would with anyone else in the same sort of relationship. Showing you the work they do and the skills they have will probably take a bit longer, but the same ideas apply.

Respect their physical comforts in the ways it seems they prefer, especially in platonic relationships. If you are in a romantic relationship with them, and your own preferences of physical comfort differ from theirs (I emphasize that I am not yet speaking to actual physical contact), you might make occasional attempts at warming them up to you—always being brief, telegraphed, and respectful. Let's say you prefer to be closer to your partner during conversations than you have found them to be comfortable with. While already mid-conversation, and while they are looking at you, choose a good moment to move a bit closer, continue talking for a moment, and then have a reason to return their space to them—maybe you go grab some drinks and come back to your previous spot. Only you can gauge whether this sort of thing might be appropriate for the individual you know.

Finally, remember that at more times than most people, a person with AvPD might seem ashamed, embarrassed, or humiliated, even in one-on-one conversation. Some, not all, may become outwardly defensive when these feelings are caused by perceived criticism. When you notice their discomfort, whether it includes defensiveness, or just things like blushing, mumbling, and staring at the floor, you might feel some mixture of confusion, annoyance, and guilt, at what seems to you like an overreaction. Remember that their feelings most likely have nothing to do with you, and the last thing the person wants is for them to make you feel bad in any way. It's certainly possible that you touched a sore spot and really bothered this person, like you might have with anyone else, but in most cases, that's not what happened to cause their feelings. These are usually automatic, involuntary reactions to internal panic over self-doubt, which the person didn't intend to show externally in any way.

In a previous section, I suggested normalizing the way you perceive the positive emotions of anxious people by treating them as if they were a bit more intense than the person outwardly displays, to match how they likely feel inside. Try the opposite approach when it comes to their reactions of shame, and treat them as if they're milder than they appear. It's a bit different, because they probably really do feel as much shame as they're displaying, or even more. However, they don't desire to have or show these feelings, like they do with positive emotions. They likely believe, as you might, that their feelings are an overreaction, or don't make sense in the context at all; but, because of the experience patterns that caused their personality disorder, they feel ashamed anyway. You don't need to ignore the shame reaction—just interpret it as being somewhat less intense than it seems to you, and respond to that as you would.

You should never feel like you're walking on eggshells around someone with AvPD. Not only is that a horrible feeling for you, which no one should expect you to put yourself through, but people with AvPD

213

overwhelmingly do *not* want you to feel that way around us. Our frequent feelings of shame are a fact of our life—we can't avoid them, even when we're completely alone. When we show them, it is not a sign that you are doing something wrong.

Most of us want to have normal relationships, in which we can talk about the same things that everyone else does. We often feel like we can't have these relationships, because we either know or assume that our shame is making other people uncomfortable—which is the most shameful feeling that there is. If you are in a close relationship with someone with AvPD, understand the true reasons for their shame, accept that it will show sometimes, and when it does, trust that it doesn't speak to how they feel about you.

The final set of hurdles I want to mention includes issues of external emotional presence. The person with AvPD whom you care about is possibly deeply emotional, but is very likely to be uncomfortable conveying most emotions to others. My range of verbal emotional expression generally includes neutrality, amusement, resignation, and real or feigned irritation, each sometimes displayed through sarcasm. Internally, though, I often feel a wide variety of intense emotions. Depending on the sort of relationship you're in, there are two or three ways in which the person's hesitance to be emotionally expressive will be quite obvious.

The first is in expressions of empathy. I mentioned this in an earlier section, but as you might expect, it will be more clear, and more frustrating, in a close relationship than it would be with an acquaintance. Particularly with someone whom I'm in a close relationship with, I am extremely empathetic to the difficulties they have. In spite of the empathy I have, trying to express it leaves me feeling disgustingly disingenuous. I feel like no one has ever believed that I care about them; why would it be any different this time? If I try to express that I do, they'll just feel like I'm lying to their face, trying to trick or manipulate them. It makes me feel sick to try, and I can barely manage words; so, of course, then people really do think that I don't care about them.

It seems, in my moment of panic, it would still be better to say whatever I can manage—which is usually either self-deprecation, in an attempt to make them feel like they're still handling their problem better than I would have, or a desperate offering of advice, suggestion, or solution. I immediately feel like a moron —fully aware that all they wanted was understanding and comfort, yet, in my inability to verbally offer any, saying something that makes it seem like I'm unable to empathize.

You'll also notice an inversion of the same issue when you offer them any praise, as I also brought up earlier. Compliment or congratulate them, and their outward reaction might make it seem like they barely heard you. The reality is that it probably made their day or week, and they'll remember what you said for a long time, but they might have a hard time giving you the opportunity to see and appreciate how good you made them feel.

Coming from someone they're close to, they probably trust that you genuinely mean what you're saying, but that doesn't necessarily mean they believe you're right. Even if they do, some people with AvPD tend to feel like they're being egotistical anytime they feel good about themselves at all, and then they feel guilty. Maybe this is a terrible analogy, but it feels like my negative self-image is in a constant tug-of-war with any praise I receive. Any time I receive a compliment, it feels like a huge tug on that side of the rope; it makes me feel so much better. At the same time, it's a really long rope, and my shitty self-esteem has been winning for years, so it's going to take a while before I can start feeling good about myself overall.

If it's applicable to the type of relationship you have with this person, you may notice that they are similarly uncomfortable expressing emotion through physical contact—or really, just experiencing physical contact of any kind. The extent of difficulties will likely vary, perhaps depending on whether the relationship is platonic or romantic, but there's a good chance they will present themselves. Personally, even quick hugs with immediate family members make me feel nauseous, and I avoid them as much as possible; I have never hugged a friend, and the only time I can remember being hugged by someone I wasn't related to was at my grandmother's funeral, which was anything but my idea. Theoretically, I really enjoy the idea of physical affection, but in practice, it's a struggle.

These obstacles are pretty similar to the trust issues I outlined, but where those were a combination of internal beliefs and outward sharing of information, these are all about external expressions of emotion. Fortunately, I believe that they also share the ability to be significantly overcome, at least on a per-individual basis. If you want to help them develop comfort with physical contact, ask them what they want before you try, and respect their answer. "Would you like a hug?"

For a while, try to ask them while you're both in an outwardly good mood, more as a nice thing to do than as a gesture of comfort for either one of you, and they're more likely to start to associate physical contact with being happy.

Praise can be approached in a similar way, if they have trouble outwardly appreciating it: if you have something nice you'd like to say to them, say it. Then, occasionally try asking them how it makes them feel to hear you say that, using positive facial expressions and tone of voice, and you'll probably get the sort of answer you'd like to hear (though perhaps with an accompaniment of self-doubt). Eventually, they might start expecting the happy feeling you bring out in them, causing their natural response to become more positive. Building their confidence to show empathy, much like improving the disorder overall, is going to require a lot of work from them, and your ability to speed the process up is limited. If I had to suggest one thing, it would be to take the chances you get to tell them, and show them, that you trust them. Trust that they will find the words to say some day.

I don't know if anyone will ever find any real use or meaning in the things I tried to say in this chapter, but it means a lot to me that you'd care enough about what people with AvPD are dealing with that you'd read it. At the end of the day, it's up to us to better ourselves—the next and final chapter of this book is about my next steps; the self-improvements I'm making now, and working towards; the ways in which my goals for life have shifted; and my humble advice for other people with avoidant personality disorder who are trying to move forward.

But first, there's a very important final question I want to answer for you: someone without AvPD, who (theoretically) cares a lot about a person who has the disorder. If this person's progress might slow down, or even revert, and the disorder might affect them in some ways forever, how can I tell if they're trying as hard as they can, right now? I think it's an important question; maybe you're trying to decide if they need a push in the right direction, or maybe you have to make a hard decision about whether it's time to move on with your life.

Sometimes, they just can't seem to get anywhere, and all they want is a family member who cares about them to help them make it through the day. Sometimes, something clicks unconsciously, and they make shocking progress. I don't have an objectively correct answer. But I did think—with a blend of practicality and hope—of a list of changes that I hope someone will have the chance to see in me, someday soon.

I hope they'll see that my anxious maladaptations stay, but that they also sometimes go. I hope they'll notice that I make fun of myself less every day; that I do it a little more to amuse myself, and a little less because I hate myself. I hope they're proud to see me sounding and acting a little more confidently. I hope they're happy to learn a little bit more about the things I like, because I can share with them instead of changing the subject. I hope they'll notice I don't seem to mind as much when they speak to me while standing at a distance that's normal for them. I hope they'll hear me thanking them for sharing with me their kindness, instead of apologizing for taking it. I hope they won't have to assume that I care about their problems, because I'll make sure they know. I hope they'll see that I feel better in every way when I'm around them, and I hope I can make them feel the same way about myself, at least sometimes. I hope they'll know I trust them.

READY OR NOT ...

Here I am, writing the last chapter of this book, and the next chapter in my life. After so long, I have a plan; I know what I want to do, and what I have to do. I don't know that I'll succeed, but I know that I'm going to try really fucking hard. So here, I'm going to lay out the path I'm going to try to follow into the rest of my life; a cliffhanger ending, if you will, to the story I've shared with you here. If you are struggling with AvPD too, I want to tell you everything I've thought about that might help you—not as a medical professional, or as someone that thinks they've beaten their disorder; just as someone that's fighting to live their life, like you. Compared to everything you're dealing with, I know it's not much.

In my experience, surviving AvPD is about knowing your limits—knowing how they change, for better and for worse, with every passing day—and clinging to them. Some days, it feels like you can accomplish literally nothing. But on those days, tolerating the company of your overactive, anxious, depressed, lonely mind is an accomplishment. I don't say that with the expectation that you'll find it encouraging—maybe you will, but personally I don't. It's just a reality of my life that I've had to accept.

I've thought a lot about how—after feeling like this almost every single day for six years—I suddenly found the strength to start slowly pushing forward. I want to stop feeling the effects of impostor syndrome—wondering if I actually haven't had a disorder this whole time; wondering if I really am just lazy, and now I'm just getting bored of doing nothing—because my disorder is real. I want to tell you what I changed in my mindset that allowed me to start making progress. Unfortunately, I've come to the conclusion that it's yet another thing that happened to me that I had little to no control over. It doesn't just feel like strength; it comes from desperation. A bunch of small realizations coalesced to form the understanding that I can't live the way I have been any longer. I need to be self-sufficient, and I need to form new, healthy relationships. I realized that this is possible, even for me, and then I realized that my general anxiety is only going to increase until I make it happen.

I don't know if you can make yourself feel this way. I think it would have to come naturally, through understanding of yourself that I can't provide you. I can't guarantee that you would even want to. But it's important to feel ready for whenever it may come. The most critical thing for me to accept was that better days shouldn't be easier days. If you're feeling a bit more confident today, it's time to push forward, in whatever way, and to whatever degree, you can just barely manage. You might feel even better tomorrow, but you might also feel worse again. Every bit of progress you can make will allow you to trust yourself just a little bit more, raising the floor and the ceiling of your possibilities.

If you're anything like me, that probably sounds like what everyone has always told you, but has never been true. You've tried so hard, so many times, and nothing ever changes, in your life or in your head. Believe me, I get it. I think the difference is that people don't know what progress looks like for people with AvPD, and I feel like I finally do. You wouldn't expect someone to learn to swim by dropping them in the middle of the ocean with ankle weights on. You shouldn't expect that you, as someone with avoidant personality disorder, can make progress on your difficulties by just shedding all your maladaptations at once and "acting normally". You will just feel like you're drowning. Anything that makes you happier is progress. Sometimes, that has to be little steps, and sometimes, it means longer strides, and only you can know what it has to be today. And, if you're honestly happy the way you are, I'm not trying to push you to change. I just know that I need that change.

Making videos about the disorder is what came first for me; then, I started writing this book, both of which have helped my self-esteem, but not without confronting anxiety and self-doubt in ways that I couldn't have managed until recently. I'm trying small things to make myself feel better inside, and while you won't necessarily find the same things useful that I did, I'd like to share some of them. I try to consider my use of social media carefully—sites like Reddit can provide much-needed distraction from my depression and anxiety, but they can also cause intrusive thoughts that make these things worse, so consider the cost-benefit ratio for yourself before opening something out of habit. It's infinitely easier to open YouTube for the hundredth time today than to make myself go outside, but the latter is often more effective at taking my mind off things, if for just a little while. When I do have intrusive thoughts, I try to remind myself of reality— the things I most need or want, and how I will have to spend myself to get them—and that my goals and expectations for myself matter, more than what I might perceive as society's expectations of everyone.

The ways I'm improving my social anxiety are still very small, because that's where I am in the process. A great example of something that may have looked like progress to others, but wasn't actually helping me, was uploading videos of myself talking. I was fighting against my anxiety, but I wasn't getting more comfortable—I was just getting by. I have been able to turn it into something that actually helps my anxiety by listening to music while recording. I hate hearing myself talk—everything about it, from the sound of my voice, to occasional hints of my mild southern accent; from misspoken words, to the things that seemed sensible in my head, spilling out as nonsensical word salad. I hyperfixate on everything to do with my speech, and I need to limit this to be able to manage any form of social interaction. Listening to music while speaking makes it impossible to hyperfixate, which means that I speak much less robotically. Listening back to videos where I did this, I feel much more confident in how I sound when I wasn't so worried about it in the moment. If I practice avoiding the hyperfixation in this way, I'm hoping that I'll start to get in the habit of just talking normally.

I've also tried to increase the range of subjects I'm comfortable conversing about. My brother is the person I talk to the most; I'm reasonably comfortable with him, and we have some different yet similar interests. I try to bring up things like the music I'm listening to, which has similarities to what he likes, and yet is different enough that I expect his reaction to be apathetic at best. It's still highly embarrassing for me to see a reaction of confusion, amusement, or distaste, but it's a bit easier with him. These reactions are normal and should not bother me—I have them myself—and this is one way in which I may slowly build comfort with them.

Oddly enough, I've been forcing myself to smile while looking in a mirror, and I've actually found it helpful in a couple of ways. Let me be clear—this is not "smile more to cure your depression!" Forcing myself to smile does not make me happier, or less depressed. But it does help me get used to the feeling of smiling. I spent years having almost nothing to smile about. I learned to suppress them when they came, so I didn't have to face interrogation—"what's so funny?"—sometimes from a place of innocent interest, which nonetheless demanded I share something that I wasn't comfortable sharing, and sometimes from a place of suspicion. Even when no one is around, I automatically bite my lip to stop myself when I feel like smiling.

Now, I'm teaching myself how to naturally smile again. Seeing my forced smiles in the mirror was very off-putting—but sometimes that made me laugh at myself, and see my real smile for a moment. I'm getting better at really smiling when I'm truly happy. Smiling doesn't make me happy by itself, but if I smile when I'm happy, I'm more likely to consciously notice the emotion. I might remember later, when it's gone again, that I am able to feel good sometimes. I've been smiling just a bit more in conversations with my family, too, without forcing it, and I think it's even helping my eye contact a bit.

All elements of AvPD are going to require the help of others to overcome. This seems especially true for issues of emotional expression and trust. I want so badly to address all of my issues, to be the best person I could ever be, before I get to know anyone new. I don't want anyone to have to struggle alongside me as I grow. But that's not how it works. I can't learn to take trust in someone, without finding someone who will extend it to me. I can't learn to express emotions that I often feel, but rarely share, without having someone that I really want to express them to. I am still considering how much something like group therapy might be able to help with these issues, but at the end of the day, I have to accept that awareness of my flaws is enough to get started. I have to know that I am still a good person, and that if I work hard to show that, I deserve to know other good people, even before I'm exactly who I want to be.

As I'm nearly finished with the first draft of this book, my first appointment with my new psychiatrist is less than a week away. I will try another long-term anxiety medication if they advise it, but I'm also going to ask their opinion on a panic medication, like a sedative. I think an occasional but significant boost is more likely to help me make the progress I want, bits and pieces at a time. Even if the doctor disagrees, I think it's important to have a very specific idea of your treatment goals before seeing someone. I'm aware that, on top of the anxiety such appointments cause, and the frequent feelings of futility, doctors are not something that everyone has access to, but I have personally spoken to people with AvPD who have been helped by them—some through talk therapy, some through medication—and if the possibility of seeing one is available to you, it's worth trying. There are doctors who are helpful and understanding, but they might seem difficult to find, as they have for me. If you have bad luck, know that you're not the only one.

The rest of the decisions I've made for my next steps are very personal, and yours will be different, but I have a strategy for making them, which has been helpful to me. If you don't know whether trying to do something—say, going to college—will be productive for you, consider four elements: the temporary anxiety commitments you make in choosing to do it, and the lingering ones; the immediate payoff you get while doing it, and the long-term benefits. Each decision we make impacts our life a little more than it might someone else, not just because of how bad or good it might feel right then, but because it might play into the patterns that cause our avoidance—and make us less likely to try again—or it might run counter to them, and give us a confidence boost. Even if we think we want something more than anything else, making it happen might just cost us too much. But the opposite is also true—no matter how painful something might be for us, it could still be worth it.

I've decided what to focus on, and what to let lie,

using these principles. I also have to be honest with myself—both about my limitations, and the capabilities that I really do have. I am going to work my ass off to be financially self-sufficient as an author, in spite of how much more difficult that would likely be for most people than a day job. I'm not up to handling a day job right now, but I've proven to myself that I can finish a damn book. I'm doing this so that I can relieve myself of some of the guilt I feel for living with my family for so long, but also for myself. I want to move out of my mom's house and live in my own physical and mental space. When I do, I'm going to fight my depression hard to make sure that both my apartment and I have an appearance that I'm happy with. No more blank bedroom walls, no more unshaven neck hair, and I'm going to keep up the workouts I've been doing for a couple months now.

I'm pretty decent at cooking, and I'm going to prepare efficiently to do it every day, even if I feel more like staring at a wall. I am going to play bass guitar more, and keep writing music, even if I never decide to join a band again. I'm going to spend more time outside. No matter how badly I want to, I'm not going to try to develop video games anymore right now, as a hobby or otherwise, because the scope of the projects I'm interested in is too big for my self-doubt to handle. And, no matter how terrified I am, I'm going to talk to some other human beings, face-to-face. Other than hopefully seeing my best friend again for the first time in years, I don't know what that will look like. I know some of the possibilities that seem most important to me: group therapy, some form of AvPD advocacy, and going on my first date while I'm only in my mid-twenties.

I'm taking risks for a fresh start. I'm going to learn to love myself, and I'm going to make other people happy. I'm not going to feign a confidence I don't have, but I am going to project the confidence that I do have: the confidence that all my fears are real, and that they're a huge part of me; but that I finally know, more often than not, that they aren't all of me. I'm still going to feel like a waste of space sometimes, but I'm going to keep proving to myself, just enough to keep going, that I'm not. I'm more proud of myself right now than I ever have been. I'm in the driver's seat now. I'm terrified of driving, but I'm not half bad at it.

That's all I have to say, for now. I'm very emotional as I write these last words. Please know, even if it feels like no one cares about you at all, that I do. Maybe I don't know you, but I've talked to a lot of people like you by now, even if just through one YouTube comment, and they all mean so much more to me than I can ever express with words. I'm a lot like you, myself. If you want someone to talk to, it would be my honor for you to reach out to me privately at jakeavpd@gmail.com, or to drop a comment on my YouTube channel: @JakeAvPD.

To readers not dealing with the same sort of issue— thank you so much for choosing to take the time to care about whatever this book ended up being. I hope it helped you understand someone you know, or so many of the people you never will, or that you liked it for any other reason. I would love to hear anything you have to say, and you can contact me by the same means listed above.

This chapter is now complete, and it's time to begin

the next. Ready or not, here I go.

Printed in Great Britain
by Amazon